The Prediction Book of Palmistry

The Prediction Book of

PALMISTRY

Jo Logan

JAVELIN BOOKS
POOLE · DORSET

First published in the U.K. 1985 by Javelin Books,
Link House, West Street, Poole, Dorset, BH15 1LL.

Copyright © 1985 Triad

Distributed in the United States by
Sterling Publishing Co., Inc.,
2 Park Avenue, New York, N.Y. 10016.

British Library Cataloguing in Publication Data

Logan, Jo
 The prediction book of palmistry.
 1. Palmistry
 I. Title
 133.6   BF921

ISBN 0 7137 1242 2

Typeset by Poole Typesetting (Wessex) Ltd.
Printed in Great Britain by The Guernsey Press Co. Ltd.

Contents

Introduction

Palmistry has been practised for thousands of years and during that time has developed from a mere fortune-telling device into an analytical science. Hand analysis can, in fact, reveal a great deal about an individual's personality, his/her physical, mental and emotional well-being, as well as inherent talents and potentialities.

Although the major lines on the hands develop while a baby is still in the womb, they continue to alter throughout life – only the skin-ridge patterns remain unchanged. It is important to realise, therefore, that the lines do not indicate what will happen but reflect aspects of personality and, just as the individual changes, so will the lines on his hands.

It is possible, however, for a skilled palmist to predict with accuracy how a person is most likely to act or react in a given set of circumstances although this will not be done simply through a study of the lines alone. All the features of the hands have to be evaluated and, most importantly, their interrelationships noted before any judgement can be formed.

To this end, the professional palmist will consider first the hand as a whole, its texture, consistency, flexibility and shape. Next, he/she will study the development of the mounts and fingers, noting all the details of each, before turning his attention to the lines of the hands. In this way it is possible to build up a very clear picture of an individual's character and inherent tendencies, particularly as a comparison between left and right hands will indicate to what extent potentialities have been utilised, developed or adapted.

Obviously, it takes years of practice to become proficient and it is not possible to detail every aspect of hand analysis in a book of this length. Nevertheless, the information it contains should enable the beginner to understand the essentials and, hopefully, have fun finding out.

1 Hand Types

The shape of the hand, when viewed as a whole, provides an indication of the basic personality structure; it is also one of the corner-stones of palmistry. All other features of the hands, such as contours and markings, should be assessed only within this context because it will influence their interpretation.

Obviously then, it is important to try and identify the hand type correctly. This may not be all that easy either as hands will vary just as people do. However, individuals can be identified as falling within prescribed categories (psychological, physical, occupational, etc) even if they do have certain characteristics not included in the specifications.

Similarly, hands may be classified into basic categories even though some features of a particular hand will not conform to the specifications laid down. In fact, these very differences will help supply the information needed to build up a personality profile of the subject because they furnish clues to individuality.

In very simple terms, hands are either square (straight sided, blunt fingered) or conic (curved sides, rounded finger-tips). Traditionally, however, seven distinct classifications are recognised: elementary or necessary; square or practical; spatulate or active; knotty or philosophic; conic or artistic; pointed or psychic; mixed.

The last mentioned is, of course, the most prevalent as comparatively few people will have hands that conform in every specific to those of a particular category. But, should most of the physical features of a hand seem to correspond to one hand type more than any other, classify it as such and treat the remainder as modifying factors.

Remember, too, to compare left and right hands as it is not unusual for these to belong to different categories.

The following descriptions and profiles are intended to provide guidelines only and do not take account of other features in the hand which may or may not modify them. They should, therefore, be

9

regarded as the norm against which individual hands can be judged: they are typical not absolute.

Elementary

This type of hand, which has a rudimentary appearance, is not seen very often in its basic form yet is instantly recognisable when it is. The palm is short, broad and solid, rather heavy looking. The thick stubby fingers are even shorter than the palm and perhaps ill-formed.

Blunt-tipped and with wide nails, the top phalanges of the fingers are usually deficient. This differs from the stiff thumb where the first phalange is more developed than the second, sometimes excessively so, giving it a clubbed look, as it is also stumpy. Large knuckled, when viewed from the back, the whole hand has a rugged, clumsy appearance.

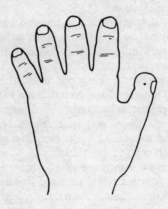

The elementary or fundamental hand is usually coarse-textured, with obvious skin-patterns on the palms which are relatively free of markings other than the major lines of the hand. These, however, are normally well-developed, deep, wide and clear-cut, denoting powerful energies and a lusty constitution.

The absence of fine influence lines or marks points to a generally contented, stress-free existence, as does the overall appearance of the hand. Often, the lower part of the palm is better developed than the top, again indicating vitality, robust health and physical strength.

The stubby fingers and wide nails imply impulsiveness, impatience with the finer details of life but an ability to grasp and appreciate broader

10

concepts. While their thickness denotes a sensual nature this is not accentuated by self-indulgence for there is no flabbiness shown in the hands.

The thumb's overall construction suggests great physical energy and an inclination to short outbursts of temper. Method, pragmatism and practicality are indicated by the knuckle size; although the stiffness of the hand shows a lack of adaptability, it does point to reliability and stability.

Even from these brief delineations (the main facets are covered in greater depth in other chapters) it is possible to see that a picture is beginning to emerge of a definite personality type. A profile has been built up, however sketchily, and this can then be filled out by a more detailed examination of each of the features on an individual hand.

At least it should demonstrate that hand type classification does provide the framework for a more complete analysis. So, what has been learnt so far?

Well, here we have an idea of a basically sound, sensible, down-to-earth personality; someone who is satisfied with his/her lot and well content with life in general. This person will simply get on quietly with the business of ordinary, everyday living, happily doing what he is most suited to with the minimum of fuss.

Such a person won't waste his time on idle speculation or idealistic aspirations that he knows cannot be fulfilled. He is far too realistic for that; besides, his idea of pleasure is a good night out with the boys, a game of football or a trip to the coast with the wife and kids.

If all this sounds a bit dull and unexciting, even a bit boring perhaps, then you haven't got elementary hands! Besides, there's all that physical energy and impulsiveness to account for yet. For this person is capable of punching someone on the nose if roused. Not that he is likely to, but the capacity is there, partly because this may be his only way of showing his frustration at not being able to express himself verbally in an argument.

Also, the underlying passion implicit in his nature will need an outlet, though this does not necessarily point to violence of course. Much more likely is that such a person will enjoy the usual pleasures of the flesh and, as he is by no means cold-blooded, ardent love affairs cannot be ruled out.

Passion apart, his strength and energy mean that he will have great stamina. This, combined with his capacity for sheer hard work, suggests a physical occupation of some kind, or perhaps an active participation in sports.

All in all then, this hand type signifies a well-adjusted personality: slow, sure, capable and reliable, with limited ambitions but a healthy, lusty love of life – a natural survivor in fact.

Square

This hand type is easily identified because, whether viewed from front or back, it has a generally squarish appearance. The percussion edge of the hand (opposite the thumb) is straight, as is the base of the palm, and the palm's width is roughly the same as its length.

The straight-sided fingers are equal in length to the hand proper and are square-tipped. The thumb is also straight, with first and second phalanges evenly developed, and is nicely proportioned to the rest of the hand.

Viewed from the back, with the fingers closed together, the hand has an overall neat, solid, practical look to it.

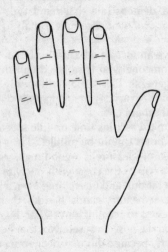

The square palm on this hand is evenly developed, showing a nicely-balanced nature, neither thoughtless nor passionless yet not painfully idealistic or overwhelmingly sexual either. There is, however, no indication of creative talent or artistic appreciation shown in its straight lines, and its compactness implies a self-contained personality, a lack of spontaneity.

The major lines on the hand should be well-marked and there are probably at least some of the minor lines and a few stress markings present too, confirming a sense of responsibility, conscientiousness and concern. The palm is also firm to the touch, indicating persistence, practicality, reliability and usefulness, though there may be a tendency to hide feelings and some difficulty in adapting to new ideas.

These traits are confirmed by the square tips to the fingers. The straight fingers add to the list confidence, prudence, efficiency and the ability to translate theory into practice, while their lack of flexibility suggests a degree of stubbornness or obstinacy in the nature. A well-proportioned, evenly-developed thumb complements the picture that has emerged by again pointing to balance.

So, here is someone who is level-headed, rather conservative, orderly, methodical and systematic. This individual won't panic in a crisis but can be relied upon to sit down quietly and think a problem through until a workable solution can be found.

Thorough, conscientious and quite prepared to work hard to achieve his/her objectives, such a person will persevere no matter what difficulties may arise. Ambition for status and financial reward is not lacking either, so success is virtually guaranteed. He may not become a millionaire overnight, of course, but at least should acquire a reasonable degree of comfort and satisfaction for all his undoubted efforts.

Perhaps he does lack sparkle, being rather hide-bound, yet he is efficient in all he undertakes and can turn his hand to almost anything that requires organisation, business acumen and reliability. So he is equally well fitted to the roles of respected employer, loyal employee and devoted family man.

Impulsiveness is not part of his character, so he won't grab his lady in the street and give her a resounding kiss but he will remember their wedding anniversary with a gift and be warm and loving in the privacy of his own home. His children will look to him for guidance and use him as their model for kindness, consideration, affection and, above all else, fairness.

Balance is the keyword; every feature pertaining to this hand type points to it. So, if there is any possibility of a wrong being done, if anything seems out of place, not quite right, the square-handed person will go all out to redress the balance, whether at work, at home or in personal relationships. He'll succeed too, for he is an achiever!

Spatulate

Whether the lines of this hand are straight or curved, it is easily recognisable because of the spatulation. The fingers are widely set on a broad palm and their wide, blunt tips flatten out to give a spatulate look to the hand.

The palm is usually thick, with well-developed basal mounts. The wrist, too, may be thick and the whole hand is firm to the touch.

Often, the thumb is large but not clumsy looking and makes a wide angle to the palm, adding to the general spatulate appearance of the hand.

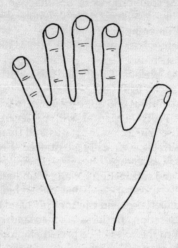

The spatulate hand can be a variation of either the square or the conic. The shape of the palm will therefore provide a working hypothesis for deciding whether the personality is more inclined to material or aesthetic considerations.

However, other features of the hand do suggest certain characteristics so, again, it is possible to build up a personality profile on which to base more detailed analysis. For instance, the breadth of the palm and development of the basal mounts point to a broad outlook combined with energy, impressionability, imagination and creativity: a very lively personality in fact.

The consistency of the hand, coupled with flexibility, again denotes vitality and enthusiasm but also a sense of realism and reliability, so points to adaptability and versatility. The wide setting and spacing of the fingers shows openness, daring and independence, plus dexterity – extroversion.

The spatulation of the fingers themselves confirms the findings so far and signifies practical creativity motivated by an overriding need and desire for constant mental and physical activity. A sense of fun, of enjoyment and humour, is implicit in the formation of the finger-tips and nails.

Individualism is marked by the large, wide-angled thumb. It shows self-reliance, originality, vitality, practicality and inventiveness, especially when considered in conjunction with the impulsiveness implied by the spatulation of the fingers.

Here, then, we have a very lively character simply bursting to find an outlet for all that enthusiasm before the bubbles burst. He/she will bounce back and forth looking at this, delving into that, trying endlessly to satisfy what is, in reality, an insatiable appetite for activity. So, this person is changeable, restless, excitable and always on the go, mentally and physically.

Although this may suggest an element of unreliability, which will be accentuated if the hands are over-flexible and soft, this is not usually the case. Impetuosity is implied rather than unreliability because spatulate-handed folk are warm and affectionate as well as extrovertive, so want to demonstrate not dominate.

Sharing will, therefore, play a large part in their lives, whether with colleagues, friends or lovers. So, should you attract the attentions of such a person you can expect to have an exciting time and certainly won't have a chance to become bored. You will, however, probably need to be spatulate-handed yourself in order to keep up the pace of this dynamic personality!

Self-confident, mentally dextrous, versatile, adaptable and enter-prising, this person can do well in almost anything which allows him the freedom to exercise his talents in a constructive way – for he is creative and expects results. Success is therefore high on the agenda whether he decides to direct his energies towards the sciences, arts, education, business or physical pursuits.

He won't, however, take kindly to others trying to impose their wills on him because he is too independent to countenance such behaviour. Not that others' interference constitutes much of a threat in his life because, with all his qualities, he is a natural leader anyway.

Others will follow wherever he goes. Which could be almost anywhere on earth – or off the earth, come to that – given his boundless energy, enthusiasm and lively curiosity because, at heart, he is a pioneer.

Knotty

Although, like the square hand, the percussion edge and base of the palm are straightish, the palm of this hand is noticeably longer than its width. The hand is rather thin through and appears sinewy from the back.

The fingers are long, especially the top phalanges, and may be longer than the palm. Their joints have a characteristically knobbly appearance and the nails are usually rectangular whereas the finger-tips may be slightly rounded.

The thumb tends to be low-set, with both phalanges of equal proportion. Viewed as a whole, the hand is long and bony.

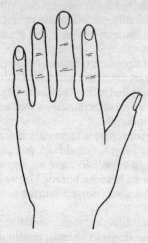

The knotted hand is a variation of the square, so shares some of the same characteristics although the longer palm shows a personality less constrained by material considerations. The elongation occurs mainly in the upper part of the hand, suggesting a heightened awareness, an inclination towards the abstract, to reason and logic for their own sake.

This predisposition to study is confirmed by the length of the fingers, especially the first and second phalanges, which indicates a cautious, reasoned approach and great attention to detail. The fingers are not usually very flexible either, again suggesting a laborious intelligence and philosophical outlook.

In fact, this hand type is often termed the philosophic, and with good reason. The most noticeable feature is the prominent knotting of the joints and this signifies a marked capacity for critical analysis, assimilation and deliberation. This is further borne out by the development and setting of the thumb, showing independence, determination and reason, combined with a persistent, painstaking search for the facts of any matter.

The general appearance of the hand suggests a degree of refinement, of sensitivity allied to dignity. This is accentuated by its thinness which also hints at a lack of robustness, so the activity shown in the hands will be directed mentally rather than physically.

From this thumb-nail sketch it is possible to recognise a profound thinker with a strongly analytical mind. The basic hand-shape is square not round, so this is no idle dreamer but a researcher, a seeker of facts not fantasies; someone who takes nothing for granted but who must work everything out for himself/herself and does so, slowly but surely.

This preoccupation with the realms of the mind makes him rather aloof and others may find him unapproachable, believing him to be cold and uncaring. Yet such an appraisal is belied by the extreme sensitivity shown in the hands. So this person certainly does have feelings, very deep ones, but has a tendency to shy away from public displays of emotion of any kind.

He is not demonstrative in the sense of being overtly sexual, nor will he shout and rave, for he is slow to anger. Yet he will never forget a slight or injury done to him and will feel deeply hurt by it. He is also romantic and very sincere, so tends to be a sentimental lover and is loyal to his friends.

Traditionally, people with this type of hand are labelled as 'religious' because they love wisdom and may well be attracted to mystery or mysticism. Yet this assumption of spirituality should not be made unless other features in the hand tend to support it. Perhaps a better description would be 'dedicated' or 'devoted' which could, of course, be applied to numerous causes including science and education which are just as likely.

Ironically enough, in view of his innate idealism, such a person often is materially successful. He is, after all, ambitious in the sense of being strongly motivated.

Patient and persistent, he is continually garnering information, assimilating knowledge, weighing facts, questioning the validity of all things in his sheer determination to get to the root of a matter. Indeed the eternal seeker after truth, he is an independent thinker.

Conic

The lines of this hand are curved, even the base of the palm may have a slightly rounded look, but no heaviness is apparent. Viewed from the back, the hand starts from a narrow wrist, bulges out at the palm and narrows in again towards the finger-tips.

The fingers, which are smooth and tapering, end in gently rounded tips and are normally the same length as the palm. The thumb also tapers to an oval tip and is pliable, making an easy angle to the hand.

Altogether, the conic hand has a smooth, refined appearance and may be quite soft to the touch.

17

This is a very different type of hand to the other basic shape, the square. All its lines are smooth, gently rounded so as to give a softer, more feminine quality. This is its main characteristic; it is a receptive rather than an active hand.

The roundness to the base and outer edge of the palm denotes imagination, aesthetic appreciation and creativity. A conic-handed person is therefore motivated by impulse not reason and will respond instinctively to impressions instead of acting or reacting as a result of premeditation.

Receptivity and sensitivity are also marked by the conic fingers, signifying an instinctive response to external stimuli. Their smoothness suggests impulsiveness, restlessness and adaptability, someone who is impatient and eager for change and variety.

The pliability of the thumb reflects that of the personality and this trait is certainly likely to be a dominant one in a conic-handed individual. Extroversion, generosity, emotionalism and common sense are indicated by the thumb setting, implying a warm, expressive nature.

It is important to note here that the consistency and flexibility of the whole hand will colour the interpretation of the characteristics mentioned, perhaps even more than with other hand types, so it is essential to check these factors before embarking on analysis.

Basically, the conic-handed personality is very complex and capricious, hard to understand and even harder to pin down. Guided by emotion, such a person's mood can switch instantly from one extreme to the other. He/she will start something with enthusiasm and just as quickly lose interest, leaving it to others to complete the task while he goes off at a new tangent.

This trait tends to impinge on relationships too. Not that he lacks feeling, quite the reverse, that's the trouble. He is always seeking new sensations and therefore finds it hard to make long-term commitments. He is, however, charming and sociable, so can be an entertaining companion or romantically exciting lover for as long as the friendship or love affair lasts.

Once boredom begins to set in, though, he'll be off because he cannot abide monotony and becomes very depressed if he lacks the stimulation his personality demands or feels restricted in any way. Such a person enjoys occupations that give him opportunities to exercise his various talents and which allow his vivid imagination free reign.

Very creative, the conic-handed individual often has artistic ability as well as aesthetic appreciation so may well follow this inclination professionally. There are other choices open to him, of course, and he will chop and change until he finds the one that satisfies his needs best.

He could be brilliantly successful too as he can display flashes of sheer genius. Equally, he may be a complete failure, unable to sustain his efforts long enough to achieve results. He is a bit of an extremist in everything and others tend to hate or love him. There can be no half measures with him because he is such an individualist.

Pointed

An elongated, slimmer version of the conic, the palm of this hand is long, narrow and insubstantial looking. The fingers are long, perhaps even longer than the palm, smooth-sided and taper off to a point. The nails are usually almond shaped.

The thumb, too, is long, slimly tapered and very flexible like the rest of the hand. In fact, the whole hand has a smooth, graceful appearance.

This type of hand is not often seen in its idealised form yet is easily recognisable by its delicacy of shape. It is long, slender and beautifully fashioned.

Although much more fragile looking, this is a variation of the conic hand and displays some of the same characteristics. In this case, though, the sensitivity is accentuated due to elongation of palm and fingers. The longer palm points to intellectual and emotional idealism as well as heightened perception and greater reliance on intuition.

The shape of the finger-tips and nails tends to emphasise these qualities and denotes extreme sensitivity, impressionability and a gentle, dreamy disposition as well as a lack of stamina. The thumb again marks a compliant nature, someone over-eager to adapt and bend his/her will to others because there is little indication of drive or determination shown.

The flexibility of the whole hand reflects a very impressionable, emotionally dependent, highly-strung personality.

The main difference between this hand type and the conic is one of degree. Here the emphasis is on idealistic or spiritual fulfilment rather than on intellectual and sensory stimulation, so there is not the same desire for the company of others.

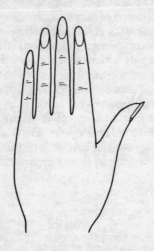

In fact, there is a tendency to retreat from the harsher realities of life because pointed-handed folk are very thin-skinned, both literally and figuratively. Hyper-sensitive to hurt, whether their own or that of others, they will escape into worlds of their own making in an attempt to avoid it.

Admittedly, such a world is ethereal, it lacks substance, but it will cushion its occupant from the rigours of everyday existence, or so he/she hopes. For this gentle soul is not very well suited to modern-day life with its emphasis on commercialism, high technology and political unrest.

Such things won't interest this subject who yearns for peace and universal love, who dreams of an age long gone when knights rode white horses and rescued damsels in distress. Yet the trouble with dreams, like all unreal visions, is that they don't last; there comes the awakening.

This is where the pointed-handed person may suffer more than most. Yet his strong imaginative powers and perceptive talents can be put to positive use. He may not be very practical, punctual or methodical, he may not want to join the rat-race, yet he does have to live in the real world in order to survive.

He does, after all, have the capacity for turning the dream into reality – on the screen or in a book; he can create real visions through painting or design. He can in fact find outlets for his especial talents because he is versatile and adaptable, with an instinctive understanding of others' needs and wants.

Very perceptive and intuitive, he may have developed psychic skills or mediumistic ability, which accounts for this hand's other title. But, no matter how he decides to use his talents, he will continue to be a dreamer of dreams, for he will always be an idealist.

Mixed

As already mentioned, few hands will conform in every respect to the other six hand types although they may share some features. This is why the mixed classification was devised.

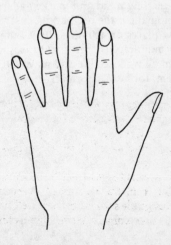

Even though any or every feature on a hand may be identified as belonging to a different category, the basic palm shape must be square or conic and this should be used as the starting off point for further evaluation. The fingers, though, can vary enormously and may comprise any combination of the available types. Other features, too, such as thumbs or flexibility, may be recognised as pertaining to a different group from the palm.

Familiarity with the hand types will enable you to decide whether a hand really does belong in one or other of the categories despite displaying one or two modifying features or should more properly be described as mixed. This is important to establish because there are certain characteristics common to all mixed hand-type personalities.

By definition, a mixed hand implies versatility, so its owner will be able to adapt easily to almost any circumstance that arises. He/she is also likely to be very restless and changeable, constantly seeking new avenues to explore, so will enjoy an eventful life full of variety and excitement.

Although unlikely to retain fixed goals for long, he is zestful and curious, mentally alert and active. He can therefore bring ideas to life for he is an original thinker who finds stimulation in concepts as well as realities.

Such a person is therefore likely to be multi-talented because the range of his interests is so wide. Although he may take time to find his niche in life, he is innovative and creative, so can be very successful in material terms due to his versatility and is well suited to occupations that cater for changing fashions or tastes.

Having a lively, questing mind and marked adaptability, he can be very tactful and diplomatic if the need arises. Just as interested in new faces as he is in new places or activities, he is outgoing, friendly and gregarious. His is a multi-faceted personality, so he will have a large circle of friends from all walks of life and may well present a different image to each of them, for he is a born actor.

2   The Mounts

The palm of the hand consists of a central hollow surrounded by raised mounds of flesh. Each of these mounds, or mounts as they are known in palmistry, is named after a planet and is attributed qualities associated with that planet.

The development or otherwise of each mount will, therefore, indicate to what extent a person utilises those facets of his/her character that are symbolised by the relevant planet. Not all the mounts on the same hand will be equally well developed, some will be more prominent than others. This may be quite difficult to judge visually, particularly if the hand is rather fleshy, so it is advisable to check by touch if in doubt because it is necessary to assess the relative importance of each mount on an individual hand.

The four mounts across the top of the palm take their names from the fingers under which they lie: Jupiter (1st), Saturn (2nd), Apollo (3rd) and Mercury (4th). In theory, each is located centrally below the finger base but in practice may be displaced to one side. It is important to determine this fact because the more centrally a digital mount is located, the stronger its influence on the personality is likely to be.

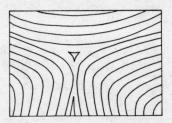 Tri-radii

If displaced, a mount will take on some of the properties of the mount towards which it lies. The apex of a mount can be located by studying the skin-ridge pattern beneath the fingers and is usually much easier to see on a hand-print than on the palm itself. The point where the skin-ridge patterns meet is known as the tri-radii and the apex of this distinctive formation will indicate the exact centre of the mount on which it appears.

A fifth mount, the Venus, is actually the basal phalange of the thumb. There are two mounts of Mars on the hand: the upper and the lower. The first lies on the percussion (opposite the thumb) side of the palm, immediately below the Mercury mount; the lower is on the radial side of the hand, between the Jupiter and Venus mounts.

On the opposite side of the palm, between the upper Mars mount and the wrist, is the mount of Luna. The small mount that lies between those of Luna and Venus is known as the Neptune mount; and the whole central area of the hand is called the plain of Mars. One other formation worth noting is a distinct bulge to the percussion edge of the hand; this is known as the creative curve.

It would be useful to bear the following points in mind when assessing the individual mounts on a hand. A normally developed mount will not look out of place on the hand and may, for this reason, be difficult to distinguish. For instance, it is quite usual to see very fleshy mounts on a

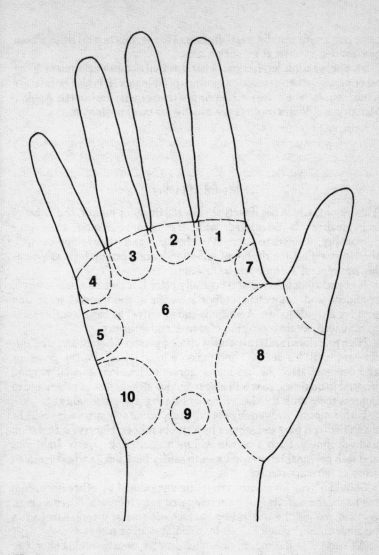

Key:
1. Jupiter; 2. Saturn; 3. Apollo; 4. Mercury; 5. Upper Mars;
6. Plain of Mars; 7. Lower Mars; 8. Venus; 9. Neptune;
10. Luna

conic hand with chubby basal phalanges to the fingers, and these would be classified as average on such a hand.

So, always consider the type of hand as well as the development of the other mounts when assessing a mount's prominence. It is also normal for some mounts to be more well developed than others; the Jupiter, Apollo, Mercury and Venus mounts are usually the most prominent.

Mount of Jupiter

This mount, which lies directly below the finger of Jupiter, the finger of individuality, is associated with the more outgoing aspects of personality. It refers to strength of character and its development will, therefore, reflect the degree of self-confidence a person feels as well as his/her general attitude and aspirations.

If normally developed and centrally placed, it reveals a self-assured, confident and competent individual with a good social sense and positive attitude to life. Ambitious and assertive, he has executive skills so may well obtain a position of power and influence.

High principled and trustworthy, such a person is honest and straightforward in all his dealings and makes a loyal friend. Warm, generous and demonstrative, he has humanitarian inclinations as well as good leadership qualities, so is well able to put his ideas across to others and to impress them with the sheer force of his magnetic personality.

If this mount is over-developed, such admirable attributes will be magnified and may degenerate into stubbornness, bigotry, ostentation and selfishness. Such a person will be domineering, overly ambitious and seek personal renown in order to satisfy his vanity and exaggerated sense of self-importance.

Should a very prominent mount be unmodified by other features in the hand, these traits will be accentuated even more. In extreme cases, egotism will be the overriding characteristic so any threat to such a person's authority will be met by calculated arrogance.

A deficient or flat mount of Jupiter denotes an unassuming character who is rather lacking in enthusiasm and drive. Unenterprising and unambitious, he is inclined to let opportunities pass him by and will shrink from publicity of any sort, much preferring others to get credit in his stead.

A little ill at ease when in company, he finds it difficult to make friends as he is too self-effacing. A bit of a drifter, such a person is basically ineffectual.

Mount of Saturn

It is not usual for this mount to be very prominent on a hand. Even if it is, its more negative attributes will be modified by a well-developed Jupiter mount or if it is displaced towards this mount. Unlike Jupiter, this mount refers to those aspects of the self that are directed inwards.

A normally developed mount denotes prudence, sensitivity and a love of solitude. Rather reticent, this person nevertheless has strong moral convictions and will sacrifice him/herself willingly for any cause that he considers just but will not countenance any form of deceit.

He has a genuine concern for the welfare of others and an instinctive understanding of their real needs and motivations. Other people are therefore attracted to him due to his obvious patience and kindness although he is not very gregarious.

Strongly motivated by a search for knowledge and truth, this individual actively seeks to explore new ideas and philosophies, so metaphysical and occult subjects appeal to him. Yet he is also concerned for the state of the environment and may take up ecological studies. Conscientious, constant and compassionate, such a person is emotionally well-balanced despite a preoccupation with solitary pursuits.

Should this mount be well developed in comparison with others on the hand, it implies a greater love of solitude, asceticism and self-awareness. Such a person will feel drawn towards religious or philosophical subjects and may develop a morbid interest in the idea of death.

Over-analytical and with a tendency to mistrust others' proclamations of affection, this subject will become very withdrawn. He bears his responsibilities heavily, makes little effort to combat oppressive circumstances and may suffer from feelings of isolation or loneliness.

As stated earlier, a pronounced Saturn mount with no offsetting features is unusual yet a complete absence is equally unlikely. The latter points to a frivolous personality and an almost total disregard for anything other than transitory pleasures.

Mount of Apollo

In direct contrast to the latter mount, the mount of Apollo represents the spontaneous elements of the personality. It relates to recreation and the pursuit of the more mundane considerations of life.

When normally developed, it denotes sociability, generosity, versatility and vitality combined with a sunny disposition. Such a person can be quite a colourful character yet has more perception than others credit perhaps. He/she can be very intuitive and has a happy knack of being able to turn most situations to advantage.

Not that he is unduly concerned with making money, though he can, he simply enjoys life and means to gain as much pleasure from it as is possible. He is adaptable, so seldom feels dissatisfied or disappointed for long and tends to sweep others along with him by the force of his enthusiasm and sense of fun.

Charming, warm and creative, this individual has strong artistic inclinations and, even if not gifted in practical terms, will appreciate beauty in all things and take pains to ensure that his surroundings are congenial.

If this is the most pronounced mount on the hand, it implies superficiality, a preoccupation with pleasure, wealth, fame or appearance. The more pronounced the mount, the more these traits will dominate.

Such a person will be self-indulgent, perhaps greedy, and very concerned with the material aspects of existence. Motivated by a desire to outshine others, he will be flamboyant, over-dramatic and pretentious or flashy.

This subject frequently displays extremes of behaviour and may be given to unreasonable outbursts of temper. Impetuous and brutally frank about those things with which he disagrees, others find him quarrelsome.

A flat or under-developed Apollo mount implies low physical energy, a lack of sparkle and zest for living: a pleasant but unexciting personality. Usually completely indifferent to artistic considerations, this person's best efforts are directed more towards business enterprises.

However, he may allow others to profit unduly from his labours without protest. Unassuming and able to endure hardship or suffering with equanimity, his strong sense of responsibility will outweigh personal disappointment.

Mount of Mercury

This mount's primary concern is with interchange. It therefore relates to information, communication, commerce, intelligence, speed, versatility and efficiency.

A developed Mercury mount signifies mental agility, shrewdness, a good business sense and eloquence. It points in fact to someone who has a lively, facile personality.

Such an individual is sharp-witted, inventive, ingenious and has an investigative nature, so may be attracted to the sciences. Also perceptive, subtle and amiable, he/she could equally well put his undoubted talents to work as a mediator, diplomat, counsellor or agent of some kind. A love of travel, of movement generally, is likely to feature strongly in his life, so any occupation that could combine this with his other interests would be sure to appeal.

Able to express himself very well verbally, he may also display literary or acting skills and take up writing professionally or enter the media or theatre as he is not afraid of being in the public eye.

He has such far-ranging interests and talents in fact that almost anything that attracts the attention of his ever-active mind will appeal – for a while at least. For this is the only problem. Although usually very successful at whatever he undertakes, he tends to lack persistence, is changeable and allows himself to be diverted too easily from his main objective by the fad or fancy of the moment.

A very pronounced development of the Mercury mount has no negative connotations by itself. But, if over-emphasised by other features in the hand, such as a badly formed Mercury finger, the Mercurian attributes will be accentuated.

In a poor hand, shrewdness may degenerate into cunning or deceit, versatility be replaced by unreliability, ingenuity develop into dishonesty and so on. Mercurial qualities are diverse and may, therefore, be used either positively or negatively.

A hand where the Mercury mount is very flat or entirely absent implies a less spirited, more inept personality than one where this mount is developed normally. Commercial and communicative skills will not be marked and he is likely to make little effort to use those talents he has.

Mount of Venus

The so-called Venus mount is really the third phalange or ball of the thumb and ideally should be nicely rounded, full but firm. It is located on the conscious, active side of the hand but in the lower part of the palm, in the area encircled by the life line.

It therefore symbolises the life force that keeps open the channels of communication between the will, reason and actions. This mount also relates to the softer Venusian qualities of love, beauty and harmony, so may be regarded as an indicator of a person's capacity for tenderness as well as marking the strength of his/her libido.

A well-developed mount reveals a warm, generous nature and an outgoing disposition. This subject enjoys life and has sufficient vitality and physical energy to live it to the full. Affectionate and sociable, he also has the ability to love others and to be loved in return.

Such a person has the capacity for appreciating the finer aspects of existence and may be artistically or musically inclined. Usually appreciative of nature too, he may be drawn to outdoor pursuits or, if the Venus mount is very firm, may actively participate in sports or athletics.

Should the mount be soft and excessively full, this implies a somewhat coarser, more basic nature. This person has an abundance of physical passion which he may not bother to keep in check as he is inclined to indolence and self-indulgence.

If a very full mount is also very hard, the strength of the libido will be exaggerated in speech and actions. But, once his passions are spent, he will be very remorseful and will go out of his way to make amends.

If the Venus mount is noticeably deficient, there will be a tendency to use the mind rather than the body to attain satisfaction for basic needs. For a flat or weak mount reveals a lack of vital energy to sustain prolonged physical effort.

As this mount occupies a comparatively large area of the palm and symbolises the basic, creative forces and urges, the extent of its development will have implications elsewhere in the hand. A well-formed Venus mount, for instance, can lend strength to a weak life line because it signifies a strong capacity to resist disease. So this mount's influence on an individual should only be assessed with due reference to the rest of the hand.

Zone of Mars

As already mentioned, there are three areas in the hand named after Mars, god of war: two are mounts and the third is the central area of the palm that lies between them, the plain of Mars. Traditionally, these are read separately but some modern palmists prefer to consider the entire Martian area as a whole and refer to it as the zone of Mars. In this book the traditional designations and interpretations have been retained.

Both the Mars mounts are concerned with resistance, but each relates to a different aspect of this quality. This fact is reflected in their alternative titles, Mars negative (or upper) and Mars positive (or lower). The terms upper and lower refer to their positions relative to the head line.

Upper Mount of Mars (Mars Negative)

This mount is located just below the Mercury mount but above the head line. It lies on the passive (percussion) side of the hand, thus its main attribute is passive resistance.

A well-developed mount denotes fierce determination and great persistence coupled with strong self-control. No matter what problem may be encountered, such a person will wrestle with it until it is resolved. So, although he/she may appear to admit defeat, this is not the case because he will never relinquish the struggle inwardly or allow others to manipulate him.

Mentally adroit, he will delight in tactical debate and can present his arguments with skill. Despite his undoubted planning ability, he is a better organiser than a leader because he lacks the desire for command. He will, however, work unremittingly for anything in which he believes.

Should this mount be over-developed, it points to obstinate resistance, one who will stubbornly refuse to budge or change his point of view even if proved incorrect. Ambitious and aggressive instincts will be more pronounced too. So, even if he has to wait his opportunity, this individual will retaliate if he feels someone is trying to get the better of him in some way.

A deficient mount indicates a lack of drive and enthusiasm, an under-achiever in fact. Such a person will often accept lower goals or posts than his ability demands yet can become moodily depressed if what little ambition he does display is thwarted. Too adaptable to circumstance and too easily influenced by others, this subject is easily led astray by stronger personalities.

Lower Mount of Mars (Mars Positive)

This mount is not always easy to identify except by touch. It is located between the Jupiter and Venus mounts, above the crease the thumb makes with the palm but inside the life line. Because it lies on the active (radial) side of the hand it is associated with active resistance.

A well-developed mount denotes a necessary degree of aggressiveness in the nature, one who has the courage to face up to life's difficulties. In fact, this individual may relish them for he/she enjoys a challenge of any sort. Adverse situations stimulate his mind and this, combined with Martian energies, spurs him into action.

Highly competitive and with great stamina, he will pursue his aims to their limits – and beyond. He never gives up and if he cannot win one way he will try another, and another, until whatever or whoever is opposing him simply gives way under such unrelenting pressure.

This character is not afraid of physical effort either, for he has plenty of drive and energy. So, he has all the attributes needed to cope well with everyday affairs and bears whatever burdens life may care to impose on him with a light heart.

This mount is not very often seen in its highly developed state but, when it is, denotes extreme aggression. Such a positive, self-assertive personality is a born fighter in every sense and will happily take on all-comers.

Impulsive, he tends to fly off the handle at the slightest provocation but will just as quickly relent. Yet, should he feel that his principles are at stake, he can be obstinately dogmatic. Basically, the degree of physical and emotional responsiveness a person displays will be greatly increased the stronger the development of this mount. So, if completely absent from the hands, a lack of initiative is implied.

Such a subject will be reluctant to assume any sort of active role in life and may rely on others to make most of his efforts for him. Inclined to become irritable if his few needs are not satisfied, he is never vehement and is basically withdrawn.

Plain of Mars

The plain of Mars extends right across the palm from Mars upper on the percussion side to Mars lower on the radial. Completely bounded by mounts, it tends to look hollow by comparison and its development is difficult to assess without verification.

One way of doing this is to gauge the thickness of the hand using fingers and thumb. If the palm feels substantial and resilient, the plain is developed no matter how it appears; if thin and bony, it is undeveloped.

Another method is to place the hand palm down on a flat surface and view it from the thumb side. If the hand arches up leaving a gap between the palm and table top so that pressure is needed to push the hand flat, the plain is undeveloped; if little or no exertion is required, it is nicely developed.

The plain forges a link between passive resistance (upper Mars) and active aggression (lower Mars) and it is also, of course, crossed by the major lines of the hand. It therefore signifies the subject's powers of endurance and its development reflects the degree of his/her involvement in and ability to cope with mundane affairs.

This is the area where reason (head line), emotion (heart line) and energy (life line) meet; it holds the balance between drives (bottom of hand) and aspirations (top) between passivity (percussion) and activity (radial).

The old saying is true, one really does hold the world in the palm of the hand! And what one does with it can be gleaned from a study of the area covered by the plain of Mars.

Mount of Luna

The mount of Luna, or mount of the Moon, is located below Mars upper and extends down the palm to end just above the wrist. It signifies receptivity and will reveal an individual's emotional and intellectual response to subconscious impressions and drives. The development of this mount will therefore reflect the extent of a person's creative imagination.

If normally developed on the palm, broad and gently rounded, it denotes a good imagination balanced by reality – creativity. This individual displays initiative coupled with a lively curiosity, so is inventive. He/she will have an explorative nature, both figuratively and literally, especially if the mount is crossed by fine influence (travel) lines.

Depending on other features in the hands, such traits may manifest as an interest or involvement in philosophical, religious or metaphysical pursuits; artistic, musical or literary appreciation or talent. In any event, this personality will make efforts to expand his consciousness beyond the barriers imposed by purely materialistic considerations.

Should this mount be very prominent, originality and imagination will be enhanced, as will creative potential. But an excessively full mount implies an over-imaginative subject, someone who has rather lost touch with reality and tends to fantasise. Idealistic but lacking in discernment, such a person may be a bit of a gambler but is prone to errors of judgement.

A very flat mount of the Moon signifies a rather prosaic personality, practical but dull. Not very innovative, such an individual is perhaps more reliable than those with well-developed Luna mounts but lacks spontaneity and finds it hard to improvise should the need arise.

Mount of Neptune

Sometimes the small triangular section right at the base of the palm, between the Luna and Venus mounts, is elevated. This denotes the presence of a developed mount of Neptune and signifies heightened perception.

Like its neighbour, Luna, this mount relates to imaginative instincts, yet it also lies close to Venus and therefore shares some of that mount's qualities too. Thus its development reflects the level of a person's compassionate understanding, instinctive knowledge and power to communicate ethereal concepts.

In purely practical terms, this means that such an individual has a happy knack of making the correct decision in most situations and usually gets on very well with other people at all levels. Often, these traits will be combined with a strong interest in mysticism, spirituality or psychicism and, as extrasensory perception will be well developed, this may manifest as clairvoyant, mediumistic or psychic talents.

Creative Curve

Strictly speaking, this is not a palmar mount at all because its development occurs on the extreme percussion edge of the hand and not on the palmar surface itself. Sometimes a creative curve can be quite difficult to distinguish if there is a pronounced Luna mount, so it is best to view the back of the hand in order to gauge its development.

If the hand definitely bows out from the bottom of the Mercury finger and in at the wrist, this curve is present. As its name implies, this formation refers to creativity, so the more marked the curve, the more creative potential there will be.

How this is most likely to manifest will depend to a large degree on the basic inclinations of the individual. In very general terms, if the development occurs mostly at the top of the curve, inspirational or intellectual concepts will be the main theme; at the middle, a combination of imagination and reality; at the wrist, practical talent is shown. In other words, the first denotes the innovator, initiator and theorist; the second refers to the interpreter, adapter, developer and strategist; and the third signifies the practitioner.

So, if the entire curve is well developed, it points to someone with great creative talent. He/she will be able to give concepts tangible form, perhaps artistically, musically, structurally or whatever, depending on natural inclinations.

3 The Digits

Once the basic hand-shape has been ascertained and the mount development noted, the next step is to consider the digits as they can provide much additional information. The fingers show the way in which an individual's motivations, disposition and potential will be applied; the thumb signifies the driving force behind such application.

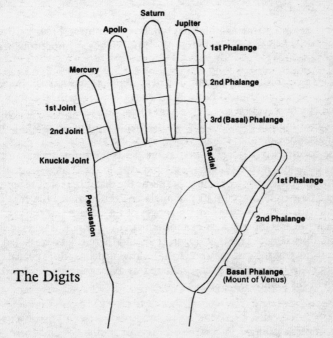

The Digits

Because of this distinction between the fingers and thumb, these will be dealt with separately even though there are some principles that apply to both equally, such as flexibility.

The Fingers

It is important to consider each finger's relationship to the others and to the palm in order to establish the relative strength of its influence. To this end, the first thing to assess is the general length of the fingers in relation to the length of the palm.

Should this not be immediately apparent by observation, measure the distance from the tip of the Saturn (2nd) finger to the point where it joins the palm and from that point to the base of the palm (top rascette or bracelet). If these two measurements are the same within a centimetre or two, the fingers and palm would be considered nicely balanced.

Usually, though, the fingers will be either long or short in relation to the palm and certain general characteristics are associated with both these eventualities.

Long   Accuracy; analysis; anxiety; assimilation; calculation; caution; patience; punctilliousness; refinement; retentiveness; suspicion; tenacity.

Short   Action; acumen; ambition; boldness; bluntness; brevity; drive; expansiveness; generosity; impatience; impetuousness; liveliness.

Having established this point, the next step is to assess each finger's length in relation to the others on the same hand. Again, this may be difficult by observation alone unless the fingers are set squarely on top of the palm, almost in a straight line, and a normally proportioned but low-set finger, for example, can be very misleading visually.

The Saturn finger is again used as the yardstick for gauging normal finger growth which is: Jupiter (1st) and Apollo (3rd) fingers equal in length; this measurement to be the same as the distance from the Saturn finger's base to midway up its top phalange; the Mercury finger is the same length as the bottom two phalanges of the Saturn finger.

If one finger is much longer or shorter than the norm, this will modify the qualities denoted by that finger. It should therefore be classified as long or short, as the case may be, in the following delineations even if the fingers collectively have been evaluated as average in relation to the length of the palm.

Phalanges

Each finger is divided into three sections or phalanges and these are traditionally associated with different aspects of personality. The first or top phalange is concerned with mentality and therefore reflects intellectual inclinations and mental activity; the second or middle phalange refers to the practicalities of life and shows how an individual will apply his mental outlook to mundane affairs; and the third or basal phalange is associated with material or physical considerations.

The degree of development of each phalange – its relative length and thickness – will indicate the emphasis placed on these aspects in accordance with the properties pertaining to the finger under study. For guidance, the basal phalanges are normally the longest and the top two phalanges are roughly equal in length.

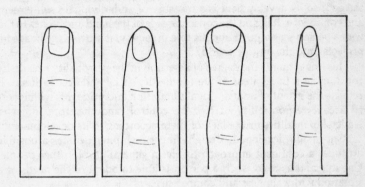

Finger-tips

It must be obvious from the foregoing that a person's mental attitude will influence his actions and reactions, so the shape of the finger-tips can provide a clue to his general approach to the matters relating to the individual fingers. Like the hand-shape itself, the fingers can be classified into four distinct categories according to the shape of their tips and each is associated with specific characteristics (see figure, from left to right):

Square Courtesy; common sense; discretion; foresight; orderliness; practicality; pragmatism; prudence; punctuality; regularity; usefulness.

Conic Aestheticism; alertness; artistry; awareness; impression-ability; impulsiveness; instinct; intuition; receptivity; sensitivity.

Spatulate Activity; ambition; confidence; enthusiasm; impetuosity; independence; originality; practicality; realism; sincerity; vitality.

Pointed Fastidiousness; fragility; idealism; inspiration; hyper-sensitivity; poetry; psychicism; spirituality.

How such characteristics are most likely to manifest will, of course, depend on the qualities associated with each finger and will vary accordingly. This factor has been taken into consideration in the following delineations of the individual fingers.

Jupiter Finger

The Jupiter or index finger is the first finger on the hand and represents the ego, so its development is a measure of an individual's self-esteem and confidence. It lies on the conscious side of the hand and relates to the way a person sees himself and his role in society; it mirrors the image he projects onto the outside world.

This finger marks the degree of assertion in the personality, the desire for dominion in all areas of life, domestic, social and occupational. It reflects the extent of an individual's ambition and pride, his willingness to accept responsibility or to take control, and therefore indicates leadership qualities or the lack of them according to its development.

A normally developed, straight finger of Jupiter denotes a positive attitude, a confident approach to life in general and to other people. Capable and assured, such a person is able to adapt to the needs of a situation with calmness and competence.

A long Jupiter indicates a good self-image, someone who is decisive, direct and ambitious. Such a person has good leadership qualities and although he may not actively seek authority may achieve it nonetheless because others will respect him for his thoughtful efficiency.

If very long, these traits will be emphasised and there may be a positive desire to dominate. Self-assurance will be marked, as will ambition, so this individual may attain a position of great power and influence, though whether with dignity or disdain will depend on other features in the hand.

Not so the short-fingered subject. He will try to avoid taking on responsibility of any sort due to feelings of inadequacy. Sadly lacking in confidence, he underestimates his abilities and is motivated more by impulse than reason so is inclined to act before he thinks.

A square tip to this finger denotes a sense of propriety. Conventional and decorous, such a person is attracted by pomp and ceremony and though a disciplinarian would make a good supervisor as he is assertive but controlled.

A round tip points to a more intuitive, impressionable character, someone who has an inquiring mind and a desire to pass his knowledge on to others. He is therefore able to project a good image of himself and his abilities.

A spatulate tip indicates the natural leader. Quick, decisive action is coupled with original thinking and there is a definite desire to be in the forefront of everything, so there may be an inclination to be too forceful.

A pointed tip signifies the perfectionist, someone who has decided aspirations and lofty ideals. Able to impress others with the strength of his high principles, he can become very influential because he is also astute.

Saturn Finger

The Saturn or middle finger marks the midway point between the active/conscious side of the hand and the passive/subconscious side. Usually the longest finger on the hand, if straight and well formed, it suggests a harmonious balance between these two facets of the personality.

It refers to stability, a sense of responsibility and propriety and its development will indicate the extent to which these traits are manifest in the individual. Unlike Jupiter which represents the outgoing aspects of personality, Saturn reflects the introspective nature of the subject as well as his need to establish his place in society.

A normally developed Saturn denotes stability, a healthy balance between will and emotion, mind and spirit, society and isolation. Patient, calm and commonsensical, such an individual won't rush in where angels fear to tread yet he will proceed to follow cautiously in their wake.

A long Saturn marks the scholar, someone who is motivated to investigate the mysteries of the universe in order to advance the cause of knowledge. Sharply analytical, he cannot be dictated to but is always ready to cede to reason for he respects others' views and expects the same courtesy in return.

If very long though, such traits may be exaggerated to the point where criticism replaces analysis, restraint becomes repression or even depression. Responsibilities weigh heavily on this person's shoulders and he is unable to ease the burden by sharing it due to an innate mistrust so withdraws into solitude and melancholia.

A short Saturn finger indicates a more responsive disposition, perhaps too much so if very short. Such a subject is not so cautious or unapproachable yet is not so reliable either. He tends to react too quickly to others' suggestions and will chop and change his ideas from one day to the next.

A square-tipped Saturn signifies sobriety, grounded on practical common sense. An upholder of law and order, this conscientious character has a profound respect for traditional concepts of morality and a keen sense of justice.

A conic tip points to a much more light-hearted approach to life in general and to conventions in particular. In fact, such a person may be too flippant if also short-fingered, so a modicum of restraint could redress the balance.

A spatulate tip adds an active imagination to a melancholic disposition. So this individual is not hide-bound in his behaviour or attitude to new ideas, yet he is rather pessimistic about the outcome of any proposed venture.

A pointed tip suggests a decided streak of mysticism in the nature. Depending on other features in the hands, this may manifest as enlightened consciousness or facile superstition. In either case, mundane, material considerations are likely to take second place to purely abstract concepts.

Apollo Finger

The Apollo or ring finger lies on the subconscious side of the hand, forging a link between emotional and mental aspects of the personality, and relates to creative expression. It demonstrates the individual's instinctive response to external stimuli and encounters with others as well as his ability to impress his personality on the environment.

It is also strongly associated with aesthetic appreciation, perhaps combined with artistic talent, so can show to what extent this trait will be utilised to gain satisfaction or as a means of giving pleasure to others. For, above all else, the Apollo finger symbolises the individual's relationship with the outside world.

When normally developed, this finger shows a nice balance between ambition and appreciation. Such a person is slow to judge or criticise and is therefore well liked; equally, his extreme tolerance ensures that he gains satisfaction from his contacts with others, thus achieving his objective – harmony.

A long Apollo finger points to an innately cheerful, confident personality with the patience needed to see long-term projects through to completion. The only snag is that he is sometimes tempted by get-rich-quick schemes – and falls flat on his face. Still, he's much too jaunty to stay down long and soon bounces back.

An excessively long Apollo tends to reflect a colourful personality. Confident and perhaps a bit brash, he nevertheless has strong artistic/creative talent but is rather inclined to expect recognition and success as of right. Such a person feels inviolate and therefore tends to take unnecessary risks.

A short-fingered subject realises only too well that success must be worked for and isn't nearly so optimistic about the results. Yet he is quick, decisive and has a keen sense of judgement, so has the abilities necessary to win through. He is, though, a bit impatient so can elicit a negative response in others.

A square tip to the Apollo finger suggests a more positive attitude. Realism prevails and talents are used constructively to produce results, for this individual loves comfort and luxury and is quite prepared to work hard to fulfil his needs.

A conic tip denotes strong artistic inclinations, probably coupled with practical skills. So this person can achieve great satisfaction and enjoyment from creative activities even if these are not taken up professionally.

A spatulate tip points to a love of adventure and an enterprising spirit. Imaginative and outgoing, this character could turn his hand to almost anything that fulfills his need to express himself to the widest possible audience.

A pointed tip signifies artistic appreciation but without the practicality to turn it to advantage. Romantic dreams and visions are much more likely to be the result of this person's creative efforts. Still, he will be well loved for his gentle kindness and compassionate nature.

Mercury Finger

The Mercury or little finger is the finger of communication, of self-expression. It is concerned with all forms of commerce, whether this refers to the trading of goods or the exchange of ideas or information. It therefore relates to intelligence, eloquence, linguistic ability, business acumen and so on, anything in fact which is necessary to enable the individual to communicate at all levels, whether in business, social or domestic situations.

The development of this finger will, then, indicate the way in which an individual will utilise the instinctive aspects of his nature in his ordinary, everyday contacts with others.

If normally developed, it signifies a good command of language, a lively intelligence and an instinctive facility for resolving others' dilemmas. This person is a good talker and an attentive listener, able to put his ideas across lucidly and equally able to absorb those of others.

A long Mercury finger denotes a love of learning. Such an individual is constantly seeking to expand his knowledge, to gather more and more information with which to impress others. And he can, too, for he is very versatile and eloquent, persuasive and charming enough to convince all the birds to vacate their trees.

An extra long finger marks the real chatterbox who will go on endlessly about this or that once he gets on his hobby-horse. Mind you, he's very conscientious about getting the details correct – so can be a bit of a bore – and thinks he knows it all – and probably does!

A short Mercury shows the other extreme, a quiet unobtrusive character who is very self-conscious and has great difficulty in putting his feelings into words. Yet he is shrewdly intelligent, makes his mind up very quickly and can be very successful in his commercial transactions.

A square-tipped Mercury denotes the doer and not the talker. This individual has good business acumen and is able to translate theory into practice with consummate ease. He has an inquisitive mind and loves the excitement of discovery.

A conic tip marks the really shrewd operator. Quick, witty repartee combined with a chirpy, cheerful manner really pays off for this character. The perfect salesman, he really enjoys meeting people and soon wins them over.

The spatulate tip belongs to the craftsman, the sort of person who is so skilled that he can make anything seem easy – until you try. Original thinking combined with practical ability will enable him to display his talents however he chooses.

A pointed tip to Mercury signifies a perceptive individual, very quick to respond to others' suggestions and ideas, though perhaps not always kindly for he can be sarcastic. He can also be successful because he is astute and his hunches usually prove to be correct.

Other considerations

Having described some of the basic characteristics of the individual fingers there are a few more points worth mentioning before considering the thumb because they concern the fingers collectively.

Sensitivity pads

Sometimes there are small, raised blobs of flesh towards the top of the nail phalanges on some or all of the fingers. These are known as sensitivity pads because they denote sensitivity of touch and of taste, as well as emotional sensibility. They will, therefore, enhance the qualities of the fingers on which they are found.

Suppleness

Like the hands as a whole, the degree of flexibility of the fingers will reflect the degree of flexibility in the nature. So stiff fingers show a rigid, unbending attitude; flexible fingers signify extravagance and a tendency to be too easily led by others.

Joints

Similarly, the smoothness or otherwise of the fingers relates to the ease with which ideas or instincts manifest as action. So smooth fingers refer to impulsiveness, enthusiasm, versatility, impressionability, inspiration and so on, those traits which call for instantaneous reaction.

Fingers with prominent knuckles or knotty joints point to deliberation, to analysis, criticism, thoroughness and tenacity, those characteristics pertaining to a reasoned rather than an instinctive response.

Inclination and dominance

As each finger has dominion over different aspects of life, it is helpful to know whether or not one is more dominant than its neighbours and therefore exerts a stronger influence. Sometimes, of course, this will be instantly obvious from observation because one finger is much longer or stronger looking than the norm on that particular hand.

Another clue is to study the inclination of the fingers on the hand. If one finger is straight and others tend to lean or curve towards it, that finger is the more dominant one; so if all the fingers incline towards one particular finger, it is very dominant and the area of life which it represents will be of especial concern to the subject.

It is important to bear this point in mind when assessing the fingers individually as it can colour the interpretation as a whole quite considerably, especially if the corresponding finger on the other hand is also the strongest.

Finger spacing

When the palm is held out with the fingers extended naturally, the fingers will either lie close together or there will be noticeable gaps between one finger and the next. This natural finger spacing reflects the subject's attitude to the outside world and can therefore indicate his general mode of behaviour in society according to which fingers, if any, are most widely separated.

All the fingers close together – This indicates a very self-contained personality, one who others may consider unapproachable due to the stiffness of his manner. Very conventional, such a subject respects authority and likes the formalities to be observed even in minor details;

the sort of person who would probably hve apoplexy if the office junior failed to call him Mister without permission!

Jupiter and Saturn fingers widely separated – No lack of confidence here. This individual makes his own mind up about what he should or shouldn't do and doesn't rely on others to tell him how to behave. In fact, he will resent it if they try to interfere because he holds firm opinions about what he wants from life and how to achieve it.

Saturn and Apollo fingers widely separated – This subject has no such clear objectives and probably doesn't give them a thought anyway. He is much more concerned with living from day to day and is quite prepared to let tomorrow look after itself. So he will take each day as it comes and live it to the full, guided by the mood of the moment.

Apollo and Mercury fingers widely separated – Independence is marked by this spacing. Such a person insists on freedom of action and is determined to do what he wants when he wants, irrespective of the dictates of society. If others don't like the way he behaves – well, he doesn't believe it's any of their business anyway so will carry on regardless.

All the fingers widely separated – A nice, warm, friendly personality this. Gregarious and easy-going, he will actively seek others' company and is willing to try anything at least once. This trait will be more pronounced the more widely separated the fingers, so there is some danger of irresponsibility, of trying to create an effect without giving a thought to the likely consequences.

Finger setting

Ideally, the fingers should be set evenly on the palm in an almost straight line although this may not be the case in practice. A low-set finger will reduce the influence of the mount that lies below it whereas a high-set finger will enhance the properties of that mount.

This will, of course, have an influence on the subject's disposition in accordance with the mount involved. The finger setting should therefore be noted as it can modify the interpretation given.

Evenly set fingers – Firmness is the watchword here. Self-assured, confident and reliable, this person has drive and determination. He is also very controlled and has firm opinions, so can be stubborn and unyielding.

Jupiter and Mercury slightly lower set – This is the normal finger setting,

44

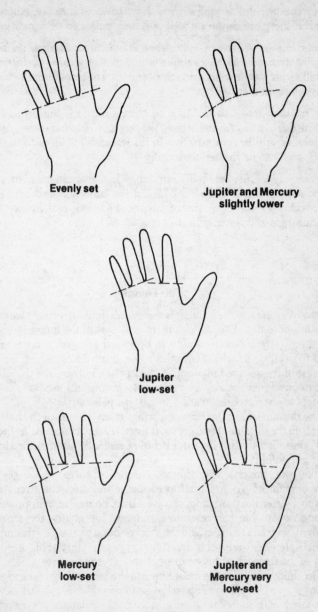

The different finger settings

the top of the palm curving slightly down towards the outer edges of the hand. It therefore denotes a well-adjusted, balanced personality.

Jupiter low-set – Lack of confidence is indicated. Inclined to be self-effacing and reticent, this subject will dislike any form of display and would rather swallow his pride than draw attention to himself even if he knows he is in the right.

Mercury low-set – An inability to communicate is the prime factor. Mistrustful of others' genuineness, the subject will avoid society as much as possible and is very selective in his friendships. Slow to build, his confidence can be shattered abruptly.

Jupiter and Mercury markedly low-set – This shows an imbalance in the personality. Such a person will lack drive, ambition and self-respect. Vulnerable to the opinions of others, he seeks reassurance in his relationships and is easily hurt.

The Thumb

Of the five digits on the hand, it is the thumb that differs most from those of other primates. This development is unique to the human hand; it is the thumb which has the ability to oppose the fingers and has enabled man to grasp and fashion complex tools, thus distinguishing him from the rest of the animal kingdom. Not surprisingly then, the thumb came to be considered the key to personality and is still used as the prime model for character delineation in Eastern palmistry.

The thumb, unlike the fingers, springs from the side of the hand. It is therefore the dominant feature on the active/conscious side of the hand and symbolises the driving force behind personality as identified by will, logic and vitality.

Like the fingers, the thumb comprises three phalanges. The development of the first or top phalange indicates the strength of a person's determination and resolve, thus relates to will-power; the second shows his/her reasoning powers, his ability for structured thought, so refers to logic; and the third or basal phalange – the mount of Venus – signifies the level of creative energy or vitality at his disposal, as well as the strength of his emotional and physical desires.

The thumb, then, is the most important digit on the hand and should be considered in relationship to the hand on which it appears as well as compared with its fellow before individual phalanges are assessed. It should look as though it belongs to the supporting hand, not excessively large and clumsy or ridiculously small and dainty, so the first consideration is size.

Thumb length

Ideally, the thumb should reach the middle of the third (basal) phalange of the Jupiter finger when it is held close to the hand. This may be a little hard to judge if the thumb is low-set on the hand (see under setting), so another guide is the Mercury finger as these two digits should be roughly equal in length.

In general terms, a short thumb indicates someone who is motivated by instinct not reason. Such a subject is impressionable and may allow himself to be swayed too much by emotion and thus find it difficult to make long-term decisions.

A longer than average thumb points to tenacity and good reasoning powers, the sort of person who will consider the implications of a project before attempting to put it into effect. It can, therefore, denote the natural leader.

If excessively long though, will-power and determination will be very pronounced so that these qualities may become exaggerated to the point of dominance, indicating a ruthless, overbearing attitude. Equally, of course, such strengths may be used constructively and other features in the hands will indicate which is most likely to be the case.

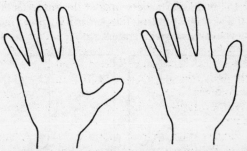

Low-set thumb (left); high-set thumb (right).

Thumb setting and angle

As stated earlier, the thumb setting has a direct bearing on this digit's apparent length but, more importantly, it furnishes clues to the way in which the individual will utilise the power implicit in his thumbs. Usually, the setting of the thumb (that is, how far up the palm it emerges from the hand) will be reflected by the angle it makes to the palm, but this is not always the case, so these two points will be taken separately.

A low-set thumb shows versatility, generosity and independence. It is also the mark of the extremist, the sort of person who not only has the courage of his convictions but is also prepared to take extraordinary risks in order to abide by them.

A high-set thumb shows less rashness and impulsiveness but also points to a less adaptable personality. It may therefore denote someone who experiences difficulty in adjusting to changing circumstances and finds it hard to reconcile reason with instinct.

The angle the thumb makes to the palm can vary considerably from hand to hand and again reflects the degree of self-reliance in the personality.

An angle of between 60° and 90° is regarded as average and exemplifies a good balance between firmness and common sense. It therefore refers to the sensible application of the qualities denoted by the thumb's top two phalanges, reason and will.

An angle of less than 45° when the thumb is held naturally points to introversion and lack of confidence. Such a person will be over-cautious, less responsive to his environment, unwilling or unable to let himself go for fear of embarrassment or rejection. He therefore reacts slowly to external stimuli and takes time to absorb new ideas or concepts.

A wide-angled thumb, more than 90°, signifies quite different tendencies. Very confident and self-assured, individualism is strongly marked and will manifest in every area of this subject's life. Forceful, determined and very independent, this person has a positive attitude and greets each new experience with enthusiasm.

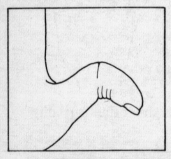 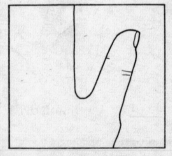

Flexible thumb (left); stiff thumb (right).

As may be imagined, the thumb's degree of flexibility can enhance or decrease the introvertive/extrovertive tendencies described by its angle and setting, so this should be noted carefully before any assessment is made.

The phalanges

Although the thumb has three phalanges, as do all the digits, the basal phalange, or mount of Venus, has been dealt with in some detail in the chapter on mounts. Here, then, the concentration is on the other two phalanges, those signifying will and logic.

The first thing to note is their relative development. Ideally, they should be almost equal in length (the top phalange only very slightly shorter than the second), signifying a well-adjusted personality, one whose reasoning powers are evenly matched by his will and determination.

However, should the top phalange dominate the second, it points to a tendency to act first and think later, possibly too late if it is considerably the longer. Such a person may be quite reckless and is liable to meet danger head-on due to a lack of forethought.

If the second or middle phalange is the longer, the subject will be strong on reason but short of the determination necessary to convert his thoughts into actions. He may plan, scheme and discuss his ideas at length, but will simply lack sufficient impetus to put them into effect without a boost from someone else.

Length is not the only consideration of course, the relative strengths of all three phalanges should be complementary too and this point should be borne in mind when making an assessment. For instance, a very bulbous top phalange supported by a weak, insubstantial looking middle phalange in combination with an over-developed Venus mount would point to a serious imbalance in the nature, an excess of drive and passion with little or no apparent control.

Ideally, then, the thumb should look well-balanced in relation to the hand with the top two phalanges almost equal in length and of similar weight; a nice straight digit with no peculiarities of form, ending in a squarish or slightly rounded tip and with a nail in proportion to its size and shape. Thumbs, though, come in various sizes and shapes, as do people, and there are several distinctive types of thumb just as there are distinctive hand shapes and finger classifications. Each has certain characteristics which will point to specific character traits.

The square thumb

The square thumb is of even thickness throughout its length and ends in a blunt tip and square nail. It denotes the realist, the person who uses his reasoning powers constructively to plan ahead with due consideration for all eventualities before attempting to put schemes into practice.

Equally, when faced with a choice, such an individual will weigh up the pros and cons carefully prior to taking action but, once the decision has been made, will stick to it and carry out the required task efficiently and reliably.

It is, then, essentially a practical thumb, denoting common sense, openness to reason and the views of others, plus the perseverance and determination necessary to see things through to completion and achieve results.

The conic thumb

The conic thumb is smooth-sided and tapers towards its top, to end with a rounded tip. More emotionally orientated than the square thumb type, this person reacts faster to external stimuli and assimilates information more quickly.

But its owner lacks the perseverance shown by the square thumb and is more easily diverted from his main objectives. He will work well for a while until his attention is caught by a new idea or undertaking and then will transfer his energies from one enterprise to another without completing the task at hand.

The longer the nail phalange, the more this person will be motivated by his instinctive desire to accommodate the needs of others and give them priority over his own wishes because this is basically a responsive thumb.

The spatulate thumb

The spatulate thumb may be basically square or conic for most of its length when viewed from the nail side, but the top will flare out to give the whole digit a spatulated appearance. Also, when viewed from the side, this type of thumb is thinner than the others mentioned, so is 'flatter' than they are.

This thumb points to versatility and its owner is able to adapt easily to changing circumstances as he responds quickly and instinctively to external stimuli. He is also mentally agile and can modify or improve the ideas of others until they can be implemented in practical ways.

Although impulsive and an instinctive rather than an original thinker, this person is enthusiastic and energetic, so will get things done because he is a doer not a dreamer.

The clubbed thumb

Sometimes a thumb will have a very broad, thick top phalange which is so bulbous in comparison to the second phalange that it has the appearance of a club or large knob. It is much broader than its length, signifying pent-up energy and little self-control.

Its owner may, therefore, be tactless in the extreme or, at best, bluntly outspoken because he has very decided views. He is also likely to display violent outbursts of temper when his tenuous control over his strong emotions gives way under pressure or when provoked by opposition because he has great determination and is very stubborn in outlook.

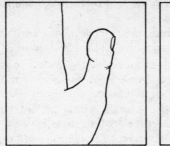

Clubbed thumb (left); spoke-shaved thumb (right).

The spoke-shaved thumb

In direct contrast to the last mentioned is the spoke-shaved thumb which looks rather like a paddle when viewed from the nail side because its face is flat not rounded, although it has a rounded tip. When viewed from the side, it is easy to see how it gets its name because it tapers increasingly from the crease of the first joint right up to the tip, so is broad but not thick and may also be long.

It points to great determination allied to a certain degree of cunning and its owner is a dab hand at getting his own way by the simple expedient of letting others do what he wants for him – not that they will realize it!

Basically, it marks intelligent strength of purpose so, even if this is not translated as physical action by the subject he is quite capable of achieving the desired end through the manipulation of others.

The waisted thumb

Irrespective of the shape or length of the thumb tip, the waisted thumb is one where the second phalange is noticeably narrower than the joint between the two phalanges, giving it a distinctive appearance.

Traditionally, this formation is credited as an indicator of tact and diplomacy but, as the owner of such a thumb, I cannot agree! Perhaps, like the spoke-shaved tip, it points to manipulative powers plus a strong instinct for self-preservation. This subject will never put himself out on a limb by voicing his objections out loud but will keep his head down during any form of conflict until the smoke has cleared, without changing his opinions one iota!

The knotted thumb

Should the joint between the first and second phalanges be very pronounced, it has a similar effect to knotting of the fingers. It acts as an obstruction to the natural flow of energy so that impulse is thwarted and the thought processes are slowed down, making them more analytical, more critical and deliberate.

If the second phalange is also thick, this tendency to slow deliberation will be intensified and, if combined with a strong phalange of will, can point to extreme stubbornness.

Variations

There are, of course, many variations on these basic themes, but they should serve as a reasonable model for analysis, especially if used in conjunction with the general guidelines set by flexibility, relative length and strength of the phalanges and so on. One point that hasn't yet been explained, though, is the comparison of left and right hand thumbs.

It is not in the least unusual for the development of these to vary considerably as the thumb is such a major indicator of individuality. So, should the thumb on the dominant hand (the one normally used for writing, eating, etc.) be better developed than the other, it points to the conscious use of inherent abilities; whereas if this is the weaker looking thumb, it shows that self-development has been impeded by force of circumstance or a lack of self-awareness or personal ambition.

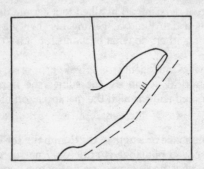

The basal phalange

Although the mount of Venus has been dealt with elsewhere, there is one point that was not mentioned in the section on mounts as it had no relevance there. Sometimes the second and third joints of the thumb are very prominent, giving the edge of the basal phalange an angular appearance when the hand is held out flat.

This is known as the angle of time and refers to an inherent sense of timing, both in the literal, practical sense of being on time for engagements and not forgetting anniversaries etc. but also in the more creative sense of having a good feeling for rhythm. In the latter instance, this formation may indicate a natural gift for music or dance and many professionals are blessed with it.

The Nails

Although primarily considered as a diagnostic tool, fingernails can provide clues to a person's temperament and can, therefore, act as a modifying factor when assessing the qualities shown by the fingers (and thumb).

Ideally, nails should be slightly longer than they are wide; slightly raised as opposed to completely flat; display well formed moons; be of a healthy pinkish hue and free of blemishes, ridges, etc. They do, though, come in a wide variety of shapes and sizes, so here are brief descriptions of the major types.

Square – This shows a systematic, orderly and realistic outlook combined with a degree of discrimination. Slow to anger, this person is nevertheless emotional and will not forget a slight.

Narrow – The shape of this nail reflects the narrowness of its owner's outlook. Not very adaptable to new ideas or trends, he/she can be quite dogmatic and rather selfish.

Broad – This points to a much more open-minded personality. Impulsive and emotional, he is quick to anger but equally quick to forgive and has a warm, generous nature.

Short (wider than it is long) – An impatient, critical temperament is indicated. Dogmatic and aggressive, such a person is very argumentative and tends to ride roughshod over opposition.

Long – A much greater degree of tolerance is indicated here. Placid and easy-going, this subject dislikes any form of disturbance to the even tenor of his existence and avoids confrontations.

Wedge – This distinctive shape refers to sensitivity and, if also very small, can denote a tendency to live on nervous energy due to an active mentality and insatiable curiosity.

Long and narrow – Patient and normally slow to anger, this person is sensitive to criticism and can react with moodiness. Sustained physical effort may be difficult to maintain due to a lack of stamina.

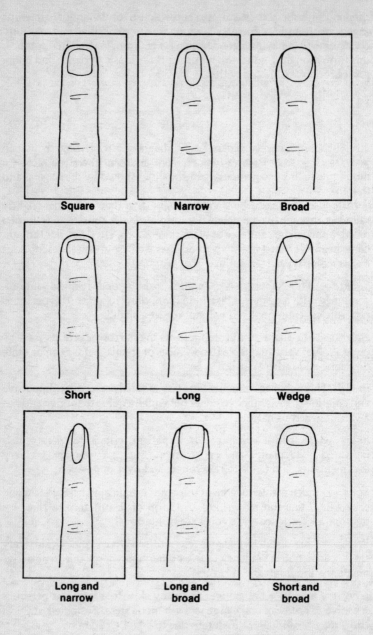

Square   Narrow   Broad

Short   Long   Wedge

Long and narrow   Long and broad   Short and broad

Long and broad – Mentally active and with good planning ability this subject may nevertheless give way under pressure due to a delicate constitution and a highly-strung disposition.

Short and broad – Great activity is shown here. Restless and inquisitive, this extrovertive personality is bright and breezy, always on the go, and can talk the hind legs off a donkey.

Finger-Prints

As everyone knows, finger-prints are used as a means of identification; they are unique, no two people have exactly similar finger-print patterns. Most people probably associate finger-prints solely with the identification of criminals yet this is a relatively modern innovation; for centuries they have been used as a means of proving authenticity because, unlike signatures, they cannot be faked and do not alter with the passage of time.

Those found on the tips of the fingers and thumb can be identified as individualised versions of five basic patterns; the loop, composite, whorl, arch and tented arch. Each is associated with specific characteristics although these will manifest in slightly different ways according to the qualities of the digit on which it is found.

The loop – This is the most commonly found skin-ridge pattern and may be either an ulna loop or a radial loop depending which way it lies. The more usual ulna loop starts from the ulna (percussion) side of the hand, so its curved end lies on the radial (thumb) side.

This formation is associated with an open-minded, versatile personality, someone who is emotionally responsive and adapts easily to changing situations. Warm, friendly and inclined to be impulsive, such a person will nevertheless have the ingenuity to get him/herself out of any tight corners that he might find himself in as a result of misplaced enthusiasm.

The composite – This is sometimes called the composite loop as it comprises two loops lying in opposite directions to form a letter S. Uncertainty is the problem here because, rather like the formation itself, this person is pulled two ways at once and can always see both sides of any question or situation.

Due to their fundamental nature, skin-ridge patterns are associated with the basic, hereditary characteristics that influence an individual's attitude to life. They can, therefore, be a useful tool in hand analysis although they are not usually easy to distinguish without a magnifying-glass whether using hand-prints or the hand itself.

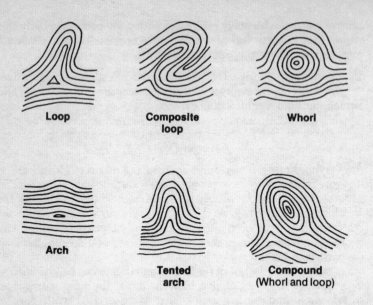

Loop

Composite loop

Whorl

Arch

Tented arch

Compound (Whorl and loop)

Given sufficient time, though, he will investigate every aspect of a problem until he can come up with a workable solution because he is both persistent and practical. Realistic, such a person has a down-to-earth approach to life in general and is not taken in by what others say but will find out the truth of a matter for himself.

The whorl – Easily identifiable, this pattern may be found on any of the digits although it most often appears on the Apollo, the finger representing the ego. But, no matter where it is seen it will intensify the qualities associated with its location because its basic characteristic is individuality.

The whorl, then, is the mark of the non-conformist, the person who makes up his own mind, holds strong opinions and resents others trying to impose their ideas or will on him. Self-assured and innovative, he has a lively curiosity and is keen to explore new experiences. He is, though, determined to live life as he sees fit and not according to the dictates of society, so may be intractable if opposed.

The arch – Although not uncommon on the other digits, an arch is not often found on the Mercury finger and very rarely on Jupiter. Basically, it refers to a cautious, somewhat introspective personality who does not find it easy to express his feelings freely.

Yet despite his emotional inhibitions, such a person is very practical and competent, takes his responsibilities seriously and is totally without guile. Hard-working and persevering, he may not become a millionaire because he lacks business flair, yet can be successful at what he does as he knows his limitations and will not set his sights beyond his capabilities.

The tented arch – Extreme sensitivity is denoted by this seldom seen formation. Impressionable and versatile, such a person may well have artistic or musical talents which bring him great pleasure and satisfaction. He does, though, tend to scatter his energies in too many directions at once and may drop enthusiasms almost as quickly as he takes them up.

Very excitable and responsive, he is moved too readily and his moods can fluctuate from one extreme to the other with amazing rapidity. Yet he is adaptable and gets on well with most people so is popular due to his warm, sympathetic nature and childlike innocence.

The compound – Although this is not a basic pattern, it is worth mentioning as it is not unusual. As its name suggests, it simply refers to a formation that consists of two basic skin-ridge patterns combined to make a third.

The compound most often seen is that of a loop and a whorl though it could be any other combination, such as a loop and an arch. Whatever the case, it is read as a compound of whichever two patterns are involved. Careful observation is needed, however, as it is easy to confuse this formation with a composite.

4   The Lines

It is important when studying the lines of the hands always to do so with
due regard to the type of hand on which they appear. The hand shape,
fingers, thumb and mounts will provide a picture of the basic
personality, while the lines will help fill in the details. The type of hand
can, therefore, be regarded as the background, the prepared canvas, on
which the lines, signifying character traits, will be drawn.

Many people have the same type of hand yet the lines on those hands
will vary from person to person; they will even differ on the left and right
hands of the same subject. The lines mark individuality, they furnish
information about a person's inclinations, talents, skills and potential;
they will also indicate that person's capacity for utilising his/her natural
resources.

The major lines of the hand reveal how someone thinks (head line) and
feels (heart line), the energy he has at his disposal (life line) and the way
in which he will direct that energy (fate line). Others will show his degree
of emotional, physical and mental sensitivity, his aspirations,
compassion and response to internal and external stimuli. Thus the lines
of the hand reflect a person's actions and reactions, his behaviour and
attitudes, the way in which he conducts his life. Alterations to the course
of his life will, therefore, also be reflected in the hands.

Every action causes a reaction, irrespective of its source, so any
incident that has an effect on the individual will leave an impression of
some sort or other which will influence his attitude to a lesser or greater
degree. This may manifest as fluctuations of behaviour which, in turn,
will leave their mark somewhere in the hands. So, the lines of the hand
can and do change, sometimes in a matter of days or weeks but more
usually over a period of months or even years.

They tend, however, not to change nearly so much or so quickly on
the left hand as they do on the right. In very broad terms, the left hand
can be regarded as passive and the right as active; one indicating
inherited characteristics and potentialities; the other, how such traits
have been developed and put into effect. A comparison between the two

will provide a record of past events and their effects on the individual and thus supply invaluable information concerning current trends as well as insight into future possibilities.

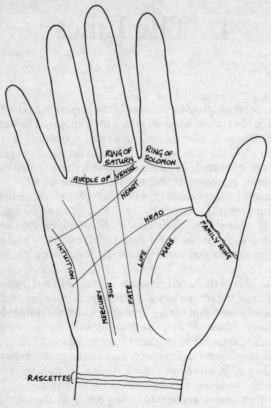

A map of the lines of the hand

It is therefore necessary to examine both hands carefully (a strong magnifying-glass is essential even when studying hand-prints) before making an assessment and to note any variations seen. Points to look out for are fluctuations in a line's course, length, consistency and colour plus any defects that appear on it; all of which will reflect changes that have occurred and provide clues to current and future trends.

In general, the lines on the hand should be well-defined, clearly and evenly-etched, and free of defects along their entire length. It is important, though, that they should not look out of place on the hand on which they appear: a very deep, broad red line on a pale, slim palm with long, pointed fingers would be just as inappropriate as a large, square, ruddy hand traced with a network of fine, shallow lines. Basically, the quality of a line, its relative strength, length, clarity and evenness will reflect the quality of its influence.

A hand where the main lines are clear and strong and which is comparatively free of minor lines and influence marks indicates a subject who is fundamentally even-tempered and content with the tenor of his life. Rather unimaginative and unenterprising, such a person will be slow to react to outside stimuli and wary of involvement. He may, however, display great tenacity of purpose and will pursue his aims methodically, competently, confidently and unobtrusively for as long as proves necessary, yet with no signs of stress or strain.

The opposite is the case when a subject has hands that are covered with a veritable network of lines and influence marks. This points to someone who is very impressionable, too sensitive and responsive, who tends to overreact to all stimuli. Such a person will probably have numerous interests, many talents and aspirations, but little staying power. Restless and unpredictable, nervy and excitable, he tends to give way under pressure due to a lack of confidence and is a born worrier.

As must be obvious from these brief descriptions of the characteristics associated with the 'full' and 'empty' hands, every line on the hand will reveal a different and specific facet of the personality. Most people's hands will, of course, fall somewhere between the two extremes quoted. The odds against every conceivable major, minor and influence line and mark being present in the hands are enormous; equally, it is rare to find a hand that does not contain at least the head, heart and life lines with perhaps one or two small influence marks, yet it is not impossible.

Similarly, although the lines should be strong and clear, this is not necessarily the case, so I will briefly describe some of the more commonly seen variations and what they imply.

A break occurs when a line which is following its normal route across the hand stops then resumes its course a little further on. It indicates the cessation of the power of that line and is a warning sign.

If on one hand only, it tends to mean that the sudden alteration to life style that such a break signifies will be of a temporary nature only, but if there is a corresponding mark at about the same point in the other hand, the implications are more serious.

However, if surrounded by a square, this interpretation can be modified as this is regarded as a protective formation because it encloses and links the broken ends of the line.

A line that splits, splinters or frays will be weakened in effect because the energies shown by that line will be dissipated: they are being channelled off in more than one direction.

Should a line exhibit such a formation as its termination, it simply refers to the gradual loss of the line's power which occurs with age.

Small forks or branches denote a diversion of the energies pertaining to the line, so may show dissipation or adaptability, depending where they occur. In general terms, those reaching up from a main line reflect efforts while those that drop down signal disappointments.

When a line splits to reunite further on, an island is formed in that line. It indicates a temporary frustration or diversion of the energies.

A chain is formed when a series of islands appear close together on the same stretch of line. This points to a prolonged period of uncertainty and has a generally weakening effect on the line.

Influence lines are small lines that cross or run parallel to the major vertical lines in the hand. They refer to testing times when the subject is under pressure of one sort or other and mark the event that triggered it.

Cross-bars are formed where a small influence line cuts across a major line, temporarily checking the natural flow of that line. Again, these usually refer to stress or strain.

There are many other small influence or interference marks which may occur on the lines and in each case it is important to identify them and to note their severity: do they destroy or only weaken the normal structure of the line? Note, too, any offsetting features or individual signs which help repair or strengthen a line. One, the square, has already been mentioned, but another quite often seen is known as a 'sister' line.

If one of the vertical lines in the hand is very weak looking or badly impeded by interference marks, its qualities will be strengthened by the presence of a sister line: a clear-cut continuous line that lies parallel but a little away from it, echoing its course. A notable example is the line of Mars which offers support to a badly formed life line; this may be found on the Venus mount, inside the life line.

Finally, no matter how many or few lines are present in the hands, and no matter what their connotations, it is essential to judge them only in accordance with the type of hand on which they appear as well as to compare the left and right hands.

The Head Line

The head line starts from the radial (thumb) side of the hand, somewhere on or below the Jupiter mount, and travels across the palm towards the percussion. Also known as the line of mentality or, in modern terminology, the lower transverse line, ideally it should slope gently downwards, more or less echoing the set of the fingers on the palm.

This line signifies intelligence, mental capacity and potential, psychological outlook, degree of self-control and powers of concentration. It can also reflect periods of emotional difficulty or warn of potential health hazards that may mar the normal functioning.

It is, therefore, a very important line to consider when analysing the hands because it will reveal how the subject thinks, his/her attitude and likely reaction to outside stimuli. First study the general appearance of the line – its relative length and strength compared to other lines in the hand – before considering specific details. In this way it should be possible to build up a fairly accurate idea of the way a person's mind works and therefore assess how that person is most likely to behave.

A deep, well formulated line denotes an even-tempered personality, someone who does not lose his head in a crisis but will weigh up the situation carefully and consider all eventualities before coming to a decision. Such a person has excellent self-control, is capable, reliable and firmly resolute, so is well able to put his decisions to positive effect once they have been made.

A thin, weak-looking head line signifies a lack of mental vigour and endurance. Its owner is therefore unlikely to be able to sustain his efforts for long periods. Inclined to nervous debility and stress headaches, he does not function best under pressure and tires very quickly. Although rather uncertain and indeterminate, this individual can be clever and intuitive, so will have bouts of inspiration.

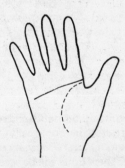

A long head line shows well-developed mental processes: intelligence, mental agility and wide-ranging interests. Realistic and practical, the owner of such a line will have good powers of concentration and may be quite strong-willed (look to the thumb for confirmation), so should be able to accomplish whatever he sets out to achieve. Uncompromising and with a tendency to subdue the feelings to the will, the head will rule the heart of this person, especially if the line is very long and deeply etched.

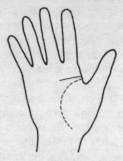

A short head line relates to someone who is more concerned with mundane affairs than with creative pursuits. If the line starts boldly then peters out in the middle of the palm it implies that the subject has ceased to make much effort, either through indifference or force of circumstance. Should the line end abruptly, it may refer to an illness or injury which prevents the mental powers from being used to their full potential; look to the life, Mercury and heart lines and mounts to determine whether the probable cause is physical or pyschological.

A straight head line signifies practicality and realism plus an analytical mind. Not very impressionable or easily influenced by outside circumstances, this individual can be very uncompromising and single-minded in his objectives. These traits will be accentuated if the line is also long and clear as this will effectively cut the palm in two, suggesting that the subject's mind will control all his actions and reactions.

A sloping line shows greater flexibility, especially if it curves down towards the Luna mount. A gentle slope to this area shows creative intelligence, a happy combination of mind and imagination, but a very strong curve will exaggerate the imaginative side of the personality and

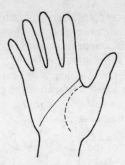

may denote a lack of realism. A head line that curves upwards on the palm implies commercial or business acumen combined with materialism. Again, the steeper the curve, the more pronounced these traits will be.

Ideally, the head line should start low on the Jupiter mount, just above but not touching the life line. This shows self-assurance, confidence and independence of spirit. Although attentive to the thoughts and feelings of others, such a person will be self-motivated, have plenty of resolution, quick judgement and a reasonable degree of self-control. He will, in fact, have a well-balanced personality and, depending on other factors in the hand, should prove successful.

It is not unusual, however, for the head line to be tied to the life line at its commencement, indicating less independence. Most children experience parental control or are influenced by environmental factors, and the length of the tie will denote the degree of dependence. The point where the lines separate will coincide with the individual's bid for freedom from the restrictions or obligations of early life. In general, this tie points to a more conservative, conventional and less impulsive nature than if the lines started separately.

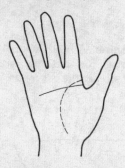

Sometimes the head line will start low down, inside the life line. This signifies a sensitive, cautious disposition, someone who relies on others to bolster his esteem. Such a person may be inclined to under-utilise his mental powers due to a lack of confidence and tend to overreact to criticism of his competence, whether justified or not. If this low start to the line is followed by a long tie, it points to exaggerated feelings of inferiority and a more quarrelsome, aggressive nature.

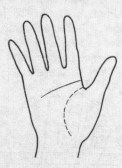

Conversely, a high start, well up on the mount of Jupiter, denotes confidence, competence and straight-dealing. The subject will have good organisational skills, leadership qualities and great potential for achievement. If such a head line also lies close to the life line, it indicates an opportunist, someone who is determined to improve his lot and has the necessary talent, physical energy and moral courage to do so. Only if this line is markedly much stronger than others on the hand will such qualities develop into self-approbation and aggrandisement.

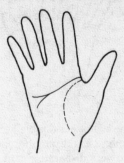

The head line often ends in a fork, denoting versatility. If such a fork is small, it shows a good balance between realism and imagination which, on a good, firm line, may manifest as an ability to put creative ideas to practical use. A wider fork implies a two-fold talent or two distinct occupations, perhaps a hobby unrelated to career; if very wide, though, there could be some conflict between opposing interests.

Traditionally, if one branch of a terminating fork touches the outer edge of the palm it signifies renown through one's career.

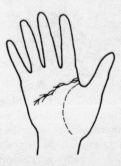

Sometimes the head line takes an erratic course across the hand or has a very uneven appearance. Such irregularities imply a changeable personality, someone who displays bouts of enthusiasm followed by periods of depression or anxiety. The nature of the irregularities in the line will indicate the probable causes of such behaviour. Chaining, for instance, relates to constant obstructions whereas interference marks refer to temporary ones; breaks can indicate illness or injury; changes of direction reflect different interests or motivations; and variations in the line's consistency can denote times of pressure or crisis.

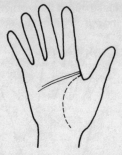

Very occasionally one will see a double head line on one hand but rarely on both. This emphasises the qualities shown in the head line and may, in fact, signify two very disparate occupations or life styles. If on the right hand only, which is more often the case, such dualism will be because of individual choice and not as a result of external pressure or influence. Indeed, it is quite likely that outsiders will be unaware of the situation unless the individual concerned lets them into the secret!

Another feature to look for is any branching along the length of the line. It is not unusual to see a series of small lines splitting away from the head line and, as long as these do not impair the main line's natural flow, they may be interpreted as aspirations or specific efforts made by the subject to improve his lot in some way. Upward reaching branches usually refer to successful attempts whereas failure or disappointment is shown by small lines dropping away from the head line.

The Heart Line

As its name implies, this line relates to all matters of the heart, both literally and figuratively, and therefore refers to the subject's cardiovascular system and emotional nature. It indicates an individual's attitude towards his/her surroundings, likely response to events or situations and, more particularly, to people with whom he comes into contact. It will, in fact, reflect the owner's interrelationship with his environment.

The heart line is the higher of the two major lines which usually cross the palm and will lie somewhere between the base of the fingers and the head line, hence its modern nomenclature: the upper transverse line. Traditionally, it rises at some point under or near the Jupiter or Saturn fingers and crosses the palm below the finger mounts to end on the percussion or outer edge of the hand.

There is, however, a difference of opinion about this: some palmists opine that the heart line starts below the Mercury finger and ends on the radial or thumb side of the hand. There are good arguments to support both points of view and I personally tend to the latter but, in this book, the traditional starting and ending points will be used although there is nothing to prevent the reader from experimenting for himself.

Ideally, like any other major line, the heart line should be well-defined, free of any impediments such as islands, breaks, chaining, bars, etc., which inhibit the natural 'flow' of the line and sweep across the palm in a continuous, gentle curve below the finger mounts. However, most people will have at least some minor markings on this line or it may be cut by influence lines crossing it from above or below. Also, it may be long or short, straight or curved, faint or clearly marked, forked or not: but, whatever its formation and course, this line will furnish clues to the owner's likely response to outside stimuli and his relationship with others.

It is, of course, impossible to illustrate every variation but the following will provide a good indication of the more usual configurations and what these signify in general terms. The reader may, therefore, need to combine several of these features in order to obtain a fuller picture of the subject's emotional outlook and probable reactions.

The 'ideal' heart line: beginning between the Jupiter and Saturn fingers and sweeping in a smooth, uninterrupted curve to end below the Mercury mount on the percussion side of the hand. This indicates a well-balanced emotional outlook, someone who is warmly affectionate, generous and out-going, sympathetic to others' needs but with realistic expectations. Such a person makes a loyal friend, a loving partner who will willingly put him/herself out for others or what he considers to be a just cause.

A line beginning on the Jupiter mount signifies a romantic, idealistic attitude towards relationships, especially close ties. Although seeking mental rapport, this individual may be too impressionable, inclined to exaggerate the loved one's virtues and ignore or deny other characteristics and thus experience disillusionment or disappointment. If the heart line rises high on the mount, the subject will incline to possessiveness; if below the mount, less personal, more humanitarian feelings will prevail.

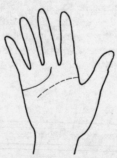

A heart line that begins on or below the Saturn mount denotes a sensual nature, someone who tends to be governed by instinctual, physical urges. Insensitive to or inconsiderate of others' needs, such a person can be rather selfish, especially if the line curves deeply into the palm. Although he may be demonstrably passionate, relationships could lack tenderness due to an inability to distinguish between love and desire. If this line starts high up on the mount, the owner is capable of ruthlessness.

Sometimes the heart line starts with a fork, one branch rising on Jupiter, the other on Saturn. In such a case, the stronger line will indicate whether sentiment or passion will dominate. If one branch starts not on a mount but between the Jupiter and Saturn fingers, this may help to balance the emotional nature as this starting point basically signifies common sense. Another alternative is a heart line that starts with a trident in this area. Traditionally, this is considered to be a very fortunate configuration, particularly where it emphasises the expansive, Jovian qualities.

If the heart line rises from just above the head line it may point to conflict between emotions and intellect. Again, the stronger of the two lines will indicate which facet of the owner's personality is most likely to dominate the struggle. Intimate relationships are liable to suffer from such strife unless the partner is particularly adaptable and understanding. However, if the subject channels his powerful energies outwards, in social or community work for instance, he may well reconcile the contradictory forces in his nature.

Sometimes the heart, head and life lines have a common source, indicating even greater conflict because three major lines are then vying for supremacy. Oddly, although such a formation points to trauma arising from physical injury, sudden misfortune or serious loss, people

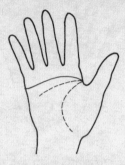

with this marking usually show remarkable powers of recovery in such an eventuality. They therefore tend to ignore personal danger on all levels in order to spare those they love or to follow a cause they believe in, relying on their ready wits to get them out of trouble.

A very long heart line, running right across the palm from Jupiter to percussion, denotes someone who will be strongly motivated by his emotional needs. If also straight and high up on the palm, it indicates an intense desire for affection, a somewhat possessive disposition: one who demands constant devotion. As this is not a realistic attitude, it may result in unhappiness or discontent. A more deeply curved or lower placed line refers to a less romantic, more physically passionate nature.

In contrast, a short heart line shows a dispassionate character, especially if rising from below the Apollo finger. The main problems arise from vanity and a self-centred, acquisitive but artistic temperament. A short line beneath the Mercury finger (most unusual)

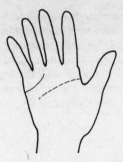

also indicates superficiality but of a more out-going kind: such a person could be very persuasive, lively and attractive, may well play with others' affections and should not be taken too seriously or will cause heartbreak.

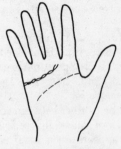

A chained heart line points to inconstancy in the affections. The owner may be warm and demonstrative (check position and length for general characteristics) yet still act flirtatiously due to an inner fear or mistrust of others' intentions. Such a formation also hinders the natural flow of the line and may, therefore, indicate a poor circulation. A badly broken heart line, consisting of a series of short, overlapping lines, has very similiar connotations, both emotionally and physically.

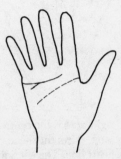

Occasionally, the heart line has a forked ending, splitting into two beneath the Mercury finger. This signifies a certain shrewdness, someone who will recognize and grasp opportunities as they arise. Charming and persuasive, this individual is sociable and good company, able to express himself well in almost all situations. If one branch of the heart line goes right to the edge of the palm, there will be an underlying need for emotional security despite any outward display of flippancy.

The Simian Line

Occasionally, the head and heart lines fuse to form one continuous, straight line right across the hand. This formation is called the Simian line or transverse palmar crease and signifies great mental and emotional intensity.

Its owner will, therefore, put all his/her considerable energies into achieving objectives. Strongly motivated and with a fierce determination to succeed, such a person has great tenacity of purpose, can be single-minded and has an enormous capacity for accomplishment.

Although there could be conflict between emotional and intellectual aspirations, this should not cause any serious personality problems unless the Simian line appears on a hand where there are obvious indications of a brutish or violent disposition. What is much more likely is that the owner will display extreme changes of mood, tend to overreact if thwarted in any way and find it difficult to relax, being so intense.

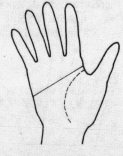

If the Simian line cuts right across the centre of the palm it carries all the implications of a long, straight head line intensified by the underlying power of the heart line. The energies of heart and head lines merge to accomplish whatever is desired, so the subject will possess great manipulative skills as well as the will to succeed.

Such a person can display judgement, may use others for his own ends and will be able to turn most situations to advantage. There may, however, be indications of sensitivity elsewhere in the hand which will help to alleviate any selfish tendencies.

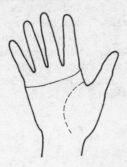

If the Simian line is high up on the hand it should, perhaps, be read as a Simian heart line. In such a case the individual is more likely to be emotionally motivated than when this line appears lower down on the palm and will put most of his efforts into securing love and admiration.

He could find that close personal relationships prove difficult due to possessiveness and a tendency to overwhelm the object of his affections. An occupation that allowed such a person to express his dramatic instincts constructively while earning public admiration – such as acting – could help relieve tension and fulfil emotional needs.

So, the overriding feature of a Simian line is intensity, though this may manifest in different ways according to other features in the hand. The latter will help indicate where the owner of such a marking could best concentrate his efforts and, as it is extremely unlikely for both hands to carry a Simian line, the other hand could be used for guidance too.

The Life Line

The life line, or line of vitality, is an indicator of the state of a person's constitution and therefore acts as a barometer of his/her physical well-being. It starts on the radial side of the hand, somewhere between the thumb and Jupiter, then curves out into the palm and down towards the wrist.

One very popular misconception is that the length of this line signifies life expectancy but this is patently not so. It is perfectly possible for an octogenarian to have a short life line and for someone who dies tragically young to have a very long one.

What the life line does show, however, is the quality of life in practical terms. In other words, it reflects the power of the creative life force and will, therefore, indicate the subject's general approach to life, the state of his health, energy level and inner resources.

The consistency of the line will illustrate the strength of the life current, the overall vitality; while the sweep of the line reflects the approach to life. So, a clearly-defined line with a deep, generous curve well out into the palm denotes an open, vigorous personality with lots of zest for living. A shallower curve that appears to restrict the Venus mount indicates a more cautious, less energetic and enthusiastic nature, especially if this line is also weaker-looking.

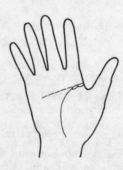

The life line starts at the extreme edge of the hand, ideally halfway between the mounts of Jupiter and Mars. Sometimes the beginning of this line will be islanded or chained and, if it is also tied to the head line, it can be quite difficult to distinguish the respective courses of these lines initially. However, as long as the remainder of the life line is clear-cut and uncluttered, such a poor start simply refers to the restrictions or minor illnesses of childhood which most people experience to some degree or other.

There is more cause for concern though if the life line is islanded throughout its length, especially if it is also rather shallow and thin. This may point to a badly weakened constitution or a recurrent health problem that limits the owner's ability to enjoy life to the full. Islands indicate obstructions of varying kinds, so may refer to periods of stress or indecision rather than illness.

A break in the life line signifies the cessation of the natural flow of that line and may imply a life-threatening incident or situation. If, however, the other hand displays a well-formed, continuous life line at this point and there are no corresponding breaks in the lines of head and heart, the threat is lessened.

Only if these and other obvious indications in the hands are present should a more serious interpretation be considered. Even then there may be offsetting features such as a protective square formation around the break or a very fine branch line which is invisible to the naked eye uniting the two sections of line, signifying recovery. It is essential, therefore, to study both hands in detail under a strong magnifying-glass before forming a conclusion.

In any event, even with supportive evidence, a break in the life line only indicates possibilities and should, therefore, be regarded as a warning signal. It is important to realise and remember that the lines of the hands reflect our behaviour, they do not provide a blueprint of the way in which we must live. So a positive attitude towards health – sensible diet, sufficient rest and exercise, an avoidance of high-risk activities, etc. – will have a correspondingly positive effect on the life line.

This is not to suggest that poor health indications in the hands should be ignored, far from it, but a sensible regime and early attention to minor ailments can help prevent or allieviate major problems. Consequently, with time, the appearance of a weak and broken life line will improve; the break will mend and the line gradually become stronger and clearer.

Although breaks in the life line coincide with periods of particularly low vitality, making the subject more vulnerable to illness or perhaps marking a serious operation, physical health is not the only factor this line indicates. The loss of a loved one, for instance, can cause a psychological trauma that will show up in the hands. One of the ways in which such an event may manifest is as a break on the life line, though this will not be the only sign of course.

Similarly, any major upheaval which totally disrupts the individual's

77

normal lifestyle, such as emigration, could be reflected in much the same way. Obviously, then, it is important to look to the rest of the hands for clarification whenever a break or split is seen in the life line.

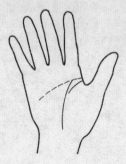

The utmost care must be taken because it is not unusual, either, for there to be two separate life lines on a hand: the original line comes to an abrupt halt and a new, strong line develops elsewhere in the hand. More often than not, the new life line will start from the head line so may be mistaken for a fate line and continues down the palm to echo the route that the original line would probably have taken.

This configuration denotes that the subject has made a complete break with his old life style, due to dissatisfaction or force of circumstance, and created a new life for himself, quite literally, probably in entirely new surroundings. I have this formation in my right hand, the original life line having stopped around 25. This coincided with a move to another country, a very different occupation and totally alien way of life.

I subsequently returned to this country, resumed a career and life style similar to those of my earlier years and the original life line has developed a branch to the 'new' line so that they are now united. This bears out the previous statement that the lines on the hand can and do alter, reflecting changes in the attitude and actions of their owner.

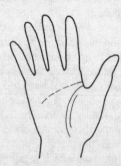

Sometimes the life line is accompanied by a sister line, namely the inner life line or line of Mars. This lies on the Venus mount, a little closer to the thumb, and usually echoes the curve of the life line proper. It may be regarded as a supportive feature as it lends strength and protection to the life line, enhancing the qualities of that line. So, should the life line itself be weak-looking or badly formed, the presence of a line of Mars will be an ameliorating factor.

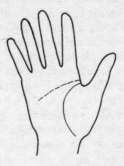

A clear, well-defined line that sweeps out into the middle of the palm, forms a broad arc round the Venus mount to end well down the hand, at the wrist, is the ideal. It indicates a warm, generous, responsive personality and a robust constitution; someone who is enthusiastic and will bounce back, full of vitality, no matter what setbacks he may encounter.

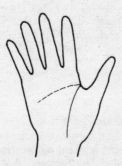

Conversely, a shallower curve which cuts into the mount of Venus signifies a degree of inhibition. Such a person may be somewhat unresponsive to others and to life in general, perhaps a little too cautious and unenterprising. The more this line restricts the Venus mount, the more these traits will be accentuated; if very restricted, a discontented attitude may prevail.

Even a life line that is well-formulated for most of its length may tend to weaken towards its conclusion, though this is not necessarily so. Sometimes the line will remain clear and strong, signifying that its owner will have no serious health problems to contend with and will continue to enjoy life right up to the end.

Alternatively, the end of the line may be very faint or tasselled , indicating the dissipation of energy, as is only to be expected with the onset of old age. The subject's enthusiasm begins to wane, he makes fewer efforts to reshape his life in any way and generally takes things more philosophically: he slows down in fact. Only if the line ends in an island is there a possibility of actual illness; though this is not of course unusual because many old people do have a short illness before they pass on, they simply no longer have the natural resilience to combat it.

Like any other line in the hand, the life line may be cut by influence lines or send out branches to other parts of the hand. Branches from the life line represent efforts made or achievements gained in those areas of life that are symbolised by the mounts to which they run. For instance, a branch to Jupiter denotes optimism and personal ambition; Saturn relates to stability and self-improvement; Apollo, expansion and adaptability; Mercury, commerce and communication.

Similarly, the line of life may fork, one branch following a normal course, the other going to one of the lower mounts of the hand. The nature of this second mount will reveal how the energies will be used. A branch to Luna, for example, implies a restless, imaginative disposition, so such a person may have a great desire to travel; a Neptune fork implies humanitarian instincts; and a branch to Mars indicates drive and enthusiasm, an adventurous spirit. A forked ending under Venus reflects a love of home comforts and normal human relationships.

The Fate Line

Although this line is traditionally known as the fate, it has many other titles such as destiny, milieu, career or environment line. It represents the balance of the hand because its course lies straight up the centre of the palm, marking the dividing line between the conscious (radial) and subconscious (ulna) side of the hand. It is also sometimes referred to as the line of Saturn because, theoretically at least, it runs directly to the Saturn mount.

As may be gathered from this, the fate line has many connotations yet is primarily concerned with fulfilment. This may be gained (or not, as the case may be) from many differing sources, depending on the psychological make-up of the individual, so it is not too surprising perhaps that this line should have numerous labels attached to it.

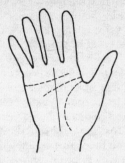

The main point to realise is that the fate line's significance is purely subjective: it reflects the degree of satisfaction the individual gains from his/her career, vocation and environment, his life style in fact.

It therefore denotes not so much the subject's ambitions as his ability to be contented with what he does achieve. Equally, it cannot be said to indicate inhibiting factors because, again, some people react favourably to difficulties, considering these as challenges, a means of testing their skill or ingenuity in coping with problems.

So, once again, we come back to the idea of fulfilment, a feeling of being satisfied with one's lot no matter what that may mean in material terms. It is very important to bear this in mind when studying a fate line and to ensure that all the information that can be gleaned from other features in the hands is taken into consideration before assessing this line's significance to the individual concerned.

Remember, too, that we control our own destinies. No matter what external influences we may be subjected to or what limitations are placed on us, there will always be options available. It is, therefore, up to each individual to decide which to take; even deciding to do nothing entails a choice, after all.

The presence of a good, clear Sun line in the hand will tend to strengthen the properties of the fate line. Additional occupational or vocational interests will be reflected by any sister lines that accompany the fate line or any branches arising from it.

If the fate line is well formulated and relatively free from interference marks or small influence lines, it signifies that the owner will realise the potential this line offers. A weak-looking line, or one that takes an erratic course across the hand, denotes struggles or frustrations, a constant seeking for a sense of direction. Oddly, though, the absence of a fate line on the hand usually implies a life of ease and contentment.

Ideally, the fate line starts at the base of the hand, between the mounts of Venus and Luna, runs straight up the centre of the palm and ends high up on the Saturn mount. The higher up the hand this line starts, the older the subject will be before he discovers his true vocation. The further into the Saturn mount it runs, the later in life will active involvement cease.

Quite often the fate line that begins close to the wrist will merge with the life line initially. Usually this refers to emotional or financial dependency which obliges the subject to bow down to parental wishes as regards studies or training; or perhaps there is an established family business that he is expected to join. Whatever the cause, it results in the individual allowing others to dictate his career path though he may, of course, feel quite happy to do so at the time due to a strong sense of duty.

A fate line that starts on the Venus mount will almost inevitably start from inside the life line which, again, shows dependence. Should this line run alongside the life line before breaking away to trace its normal course across the hand, it implies that any parental or family influence will be very strong indeed. The higher up the hand the fate line breaks free from the restrictions of the life line, the later on in life the subject will develop the self-determination to follow his chosen aims.

A Luna start to the fate line nearly always points to a varied pattern of existence. Such a person seems to have numerous opportunities for changing his career or residence and, if the line is also long and well-marked, will probably do so more than once during his lifetime. Whether such moves will be to good effect or not will depend on the line's formation and general appearance. However, freedom of choice and a very independent spirit are implicit in this starting point.

Not infrequently, the fate line will start high up in the hand, signifying that the subject only set out to follow his own inclinations once youthful obligations or commitments were behind him. A late start is therefore a mark of enterprise and signals a decisive move of some sort, perhaps a change of occupation, residence, marital status or starting up one's own business. It is the point where the subject uses his greater freedom of action to create a more rewarding life style in the future.

If the fate line starts in the middle of the palm, on the plain of Mars, the subject will probably welcome challenge so, even if he has had to struggle to establish himself, will make a great effort to overcome obstacles and improve his lot. A higher start, beyond the head line, denotes long-held ambitions but no previous opportunity to follow these through. If the fate line begins even later, from the heart line, it implies that a spare-time occupation or hobby will eventually become the means of livelihood.

As stated previously, the further up the palm this line terminates, the longer an individual will be actively concerned with advancement. The termination furnishes clues to the person's underlying motivation because it symbolises the goal to which he aspires. If the fate line forks it denotes diversification and the point where the split occurs will show the probable cause or time of this change of direction or dualism. Similarly, small branches arising along the fate line's length refer to new interests and their direction will indicate the aim of the efforts made whereas their departure point will represent the source.

The Sun Line

Ideally, the Sun line starts low down on the palm and runs up the centre to end on the Apollo mount. Otherwise known as the Apollo line or line of success, it is traditionally supposed to confer fame, fortune or brilliance on its owner. However, it could more realistically be described as indicating aspirations, talent and, most importantly perhaps, appreciation of what one has achieved.

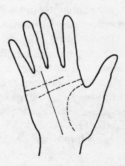

In other words, this line reflects the degree of inner satisfaction or contentment obtained. So, its very appearance in the hands points to a basically sunny disposition, someone who derives pleasure from life, irrespective of his/her current circumstances and no matter what his chosen life style may be.

It is not often, of course, that people set out with specific ambitions and achieve these with little or no effort in a very short time. So, it is unusual for the Sun line to follow the route described earlier. It is more often the case that the Sun line will start from much higher up on the palm, somewhere on the plain of Mars, perhaps on a level with the head line or between this and the heart line.

However, should the Sun line start low down on the hand, just above the wrist, it shows an early and relatively painless first step on the path to success. If rising from inside the life line, the subject's family probably provided initial help and encouragement – perhaps he joined the family business – and has continued to support him throughout his career.

If rising from or close to the life line, any achievements gained would be more likely to result from personal endeavour although, again, outside assistance could not be ruled out. A start on the Neptune mount implies a facility for getting on well with other people due to natural empathy which could, of course, be advantageous. A start on Luna points to a public life of some sort – perhaps the subject will enter politics or follow a career in entertainment, the arts or journalism – especially one that entails plenty of variety and opportunities for travel.

As stated earlier, the Sun line usually commences somewhere in the region of the plain of Mars, indicating a decisive effort to gain one's goals after earlier struggles or, indeed, a complete change of direction. Whether this entails a career change, residential move – perhaps even emigration – or starting up a business, it normally implies a new life style designed to bring greater satisfaction in middle-age and later years.

This late start to the Sun line nearly always points to persistence: a determination to improve the quality of one's life in some way, based on past experience and the wisdom gained thereby. A head line start usually refers to financial or material ambitions whereas a beginning on the heart line implies a greater concern with emotional considerations.

A forked start to the Sun line denotes two distinct careers or someone whose public and private lives follow very different patterns and are kept strictly separate. Both may give equal satisfaction although it is likely that one may be regarded simply as the means to an end while the other represents that end itself.

A termination at the head line or where there is an influence line cutting the Sun line from the head line refers to loss of status or financial failure due to errors of judgement. An influence line from or termination at the heart line indicates rivalry, fierce competition or misplaced trust resulting in emotional loss or disappointment of some kind. How serious such setbacks may prove to be will depend on the individual's expectations and determination to overcome obstacles.

The Sun line may occasionally be mistaken for a Mercury line due to their similar paths. However, if both are present in the hand, it will be relatively easy to distinguish them; if not, try to determine the line's objective: is it running more directly towards the Mercury or Apollo mount?

Sometimes the Sun line will be accompanied by its 'sister', the fate line, and these will merge at some point. This is a favourable configuration suggesting that the subject will realise all his ambitions. If the Sun line is the stronger of the two, it denotes a more expansive, spontaneous, sunnier disposition than if the fate line dominates.

The Mercury Line

Often referred to as the health line, the Mercury line usually commences at the base of the palm and runs vertically up the hand towards the Mercury mount.

Although some authorities consider that its presence is an unfavourable sign, this is not necessarily the case unless found in hands that bear obvious indications of serious health problems. Rather, it should perhaps be regarded as a helpful mark as it can show which areas of the subject's life need attention and it can, in fact, have some very positive connotations.

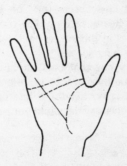

For instance, a straight, well-formed Mercury line that rises from the life line and follows an uninterrupted course to the Mercury mount, creates a channel between these two areas of the hand. As this will enhance the qualities of the Mercury mount without adversely affecting vitality (life line), the owner should have plenty of energy to pursue his/her intellectual inclinations (whether these be business interests, specialist studies, community projects or whatever) without draining his physical resources.

Similarly, a clear, unimpeded Mercury line from the Luna to the Mercury mount denotes a beneficial link between imagination and intelligence, with subsequent positive results. Another favourable configuration occurs if this line starts from the fate line and travels straight to the Mercury mount, implying satisfaction with working (Mercury) and environmental (fate) conditions.

An irregular or fragmented Mercury line often reflects an irregular life style: one where the individual tends to function in fits and starts, expending much energy on a project and failing to recoup his losses before embarking on the next. Obviously, such a procedure can result in exhaustion and irritability but could be easily remedied by a change of attitude and the imposition of greater self-control.

A Mercury line that is cut by the life line denotes a weakened constitution, especially if the former rises on the Venus mount. This usually relates to digestive disorders, ranging from a tendency to biliousness in an otherwise healthy person to the possibility of ulcers in someone of a very 'nervy' or worrying disposition.

If cut by the fate line, it could point to a marked depletion of energy from middle-age onwards, due to stress, so carries a warning to the owner to slow down if he wishes to enjoy continuing good health. This trend towards a rapid health deterioration in later years is emphasised if the Mercury line stops short on the Mars mount, indicating an anxious, over-active personality.

A Mercury line that cuts across the Sun line simply refers to a conscious awareness of health factors. The subject probably acknowledges his responsibilities in this respect and takes reasonable steps to ensure he follows a sensible regime.

Sometimes a Mercury line that cuts the head line will indicate an interest in arcane or metaphysical subjects, especially if it rises from the Luna mount. If the Mercury, head and fate lines intersect to form a distinct triangle, this implies psychic ability or a positive aptitude for the occult arts.

The Girdle of Venus

The girdle of Venus refers to emotional sensitivity, as its name suggests, so its presence in the hand will emphasise this facet of the subject's personality irrespective of the girdle's formation.

Although it is true that no single feature in the hands should be taken in isolation, this is especially important as far as the Venus girdle is concerned. In itself, it merely denotes what has been stated above, so it is essential that it should be read only within the context of the basic characteristics indicated by the hand on which it appears.

If present, the girdle of Venus is located above the heart line, towards the top of the palm. It may be formed by a number of short, sometimes overlapping lines or by a continuous, bowed line curving down towards the heart line.

It usually starts between the Jupiter and Saturn fingers and runs across the mounts in an arc to end between the Saturn and Apollo or Apollo and Mercury fingers. If very fragmented, this girdle is in fact more likely to start and end high up on the mounts rather than between the fingers.

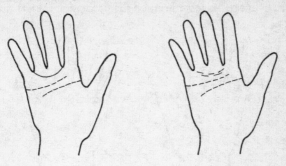

In effect, the girdle of Venus could almost be described as a secondary heart line. It may, indeed, help compensate for any apparent lack of sensitivity in a hand that is either devoid of an obvious heart line (*see Simian line*) or where the formation of the heart line and other features in the hands suggest a somewhat unresponsive, selfish and perhaps insensitive nature.

If clearly defined on an otherwise emotionally well-balanced hand, it is a mark of aesthetic appreciation and underscores any artistic, musical or creative inclinations that the owner may have. On a hand that displays other indications of strong sensuality, the presence of a Venus girdle will tend to highlight this trait and may point to poor emotional control, implying an erratic temperament and self-indulgent attitude towards physical gratification.

On a hand that already indicates a nervous or sensitive disposition, the girdle's presence will merely exaggerate such tendencies. If the girdle in such a case is composed of several broken lines across the finger mounts, the subject's emotional instability could be so pronounced as to influence all areas of his/her life.

So, the girdle of Venus simply intensifies sensitivity and, except in extreme cases, can be regarded as a helpful factor where marked emotional responsiveness is desirable or necessary.

The Via Lasciva

Like the girdle of Venus, the interpretation of this line will be heavily influenced by the type of hand on which it is found. It, too, denotes sensitivity but, in this case, refers to bodily rather than emotional reactions.

Rising somewhere on or at the base of the Luna mount, the Via Lasciva may run across the bottom of the palm towards the Venus mount or echo the Mercury line's course and run up the percussion (outer) side of the palm.

A long line in the first mentioned position will forge a link between the two mounts in the physical part of the hand. It therefore often denotes a need for stimulation of one sort or another, though this will usually be kept within reasonable bounds.

In extreme cases, however, such as on a manifestly sensual hand with no offsetting features, this trait may be allowed to develop into an uncontrollable craving for drugs, drink or sexual gratification, particularly if the Via Lasciva is curved and deeply etched. Conversely, a well-defined straight line in this position can point to a positive aversion to any form of physical excess.

Sometimes referred to as the allergy line, the Via Lasciva may, indeed, denote a bodily reaction against certain foodstuffs, chemicals or alcohol rather than a psychological response, whether found crossing the base of the palm or running up its outer edge.

In the latter position, it acts as a 'sister' line to the Mercury or health line and will, therefore, emphasise the qualities of that line. Depending on the type of hand on which it is found, this may manifest positively as a careful, selective attitude towards diet and physical well-being, or negatively as faddishness and hypochondria.

The Line of Intuition

Occasionally, a fine, curved line will be seen to the percussion side of the hand, bowing gently into the centre of the palm from the Luna mount to the Mercury. This is known as the line of intuition or line of Uranus and signifies mental sensitivity.

Although it may well reflect an interest in or facility for the psychic arts, especially if the Neptune mount is well-developed, this is not the only interpretation. It is a favourable mark for anyone to have in the hands because it is always useful to have immediate, instinctive knowledge of something or someone, no matter where one's interests lie; which is exactly what intuition means.

A long, well-formed crescent implies strong, reliable intuitive powers; a shorter, weaker line, or one that fades away altogether at some points, is more likely to refer to short bursts of inspiration. If this line's course is particularly haphazard, it may point to mental restlessness; certainly any intuitive flashes should not be relied upon.

The Ring of Solomon

This is a small curved line on the mount of Jupiter. Usually it starts from between the Saturn and Jupiter fingers, runs right round the base of the latter and ends on the radial (thumb) edge of the palm. Traditionally, it is supposed to indicate wisdom but in practice simply emphasises the qualities of the mount on which it is found.

The Ring of Saturn

Conversely, this ring formation, which encircles the base of the Saturn finger, weakens the effects of the mount on which it is located. It seems, in fact, to act as a kind of barrier, inhibiting the natural interchange of energies between the finger and palm, so may point to some imbalance in the personality.

The Family Ring

This takes the form of a chained line round the base of the thumb, thus separating it from the Venus mount. It denotes family ties, so the stronger the marking the stronger these ties will be.

Usually, there will be a series of influence lines fanning out across the mount of Venus from this ring. Again, the more pronounced these lines are the greater the family's influence on the subject's life.

If these lines reach right out into the centre of the hand, cutting across the life line, then the subject's feelings of duty may be so strong that he/she will subjugate his own wishes in order to satisfy family demands.

Lines of Affection

Very often there will be one or more short horizontal lines entering the palm from the extreme percussion edge of the hand. Traditionally known as marriage lines, they always refer to strong attachments but not necessarily marriage.

As these lines traverse the Mercury mount and may lie anywhere between the base of the Mercury finger and the heart line, they can relate to any alliance that leaves a lasting impression on the subject, whether a romantic attachment, firm friendship or business partnership.

Although such lines usually indicate personal relationships, they may sometimes apply to a love for a particular place or country or strong emotional feelings for animals. In general terms, lines that curve down towards or send influence lines to the heart line show romantic attachments whereas those that go towards the Mercury finger relate to less passionate relationships.

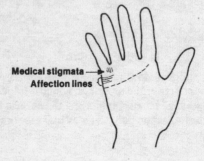

Medical stigmata

Affection lines

Medical Stigmata

Sometimes there will be three or four short vertical lines high up on the Mercury mount, just below the base of that finger and to one side of it. These are referred to as the medical stigmata or Samaritan lines and indicate a compassionate nature and aptitude for healing.

The person with these marks on his/her hands may well take up a medical career or enter one of the caring professions if other indications in the hands tend to confirm this. At the very least, the stigmata reflect an interest in health or healing combined with a strong desire to help others.

The Rascettes

The rascettes, or bracelets as they are sometimes called, are the horizontal lines that cross the inside of the wrist, below the palm. Their number can vary from one to four although two or three is average.

Traditionally, they are supposed to refer to longevity although it would be truer to regard them as indicators of the subject's physical well-being. The first rascette, that is the one closest to the palm, is of prime signficance in this respect.

If this rascette is clearly-defined and deeply etched it implies good health and vitality. However, if this bracelet arches up to such an extent that it invades the palm, it indicates the possibility of some weakness in the genito-urinary system.

This may manifest as bladder or menstrual problems and should, therefore, be carefully noted in a woman's hands as foreknowledge could lead to remedial treatment and thus help prevent later complications. The probability of such difficulties arising is magnified if the second rascette also arches up into the palm.

Getting away from health matters, often there will be a series of fine lines running up the palm from the rascettes and these relate to journeys. The more numerous the lines, the more likely the subject is to travel; the longer the lines, the longer such journeys will be.

Besides the fine lines that traverse the Luna mount from the rascettes, similar travel lines may be seen to enter the palm vertically from the percussion edge of the hand, below the level of the head line. Traditionally, if the ends of such lines turn up, the journeys undertaken will prove satisfactory, whereas if they turn down, disappointment is indicated.

Incidentals

It is quite usual to see dots, cross-bars or islands on the lines of the hand. These chance markings all impede the progress of a line in some way and therefore have a weakening or inhibiting effect on the power of the line on which they are found.

In every case, the effects of such interference will be of a temporary nature, lasting only as long as the defect itself persists. Dots and bars are therefore of a very transitory nature whereas a large island may refer to a period of several months or years depending on the properties of the line on which it appears.

Dots and bars may be considered as obstacles, perhaps minor difficulties or delays in the matters governed by the line. A bar's influence is stronger than that of a dot, signifying that the subject may experience greater difficulty in overcoming whatever problem or setback is manifest.

Islands have more serious implications, especially if on one of the major lines. An island has a debilitating effect on the power of any line on which it appears and must, therefore, be interpreted only in accordance with the properties of that line. For instance, a large island on the life line refers to a weakened constitution, perhaps as a result of illness or accident.

It is important to study the rest of the hand, however, in order to identify the probable cause of islanding and to take note of the line's condition beyond the point where such a marking terminates. If the line is weaker looking thereafter, it could indicate a poor or slow recovery from the effects of the islanding; whereas a strong, clear continuation of the line points to the complete restoration of the energies associated with whichever line is involved.

Dots, bars and islands have significance only if falling on a line but there are other meaningful formations which may occur on a line or elsewhere in the hand.

A grille, for instance, has similar implications to an island although it may appear on a mount or a line. In fact, this is most commonly found on a mount, notably the Venus, and denotes a dissipation of the energies pertaining to the site where it is found.

A square, on the other hand (no pun intended!), is always a favourable sign, indicating the preservation or enhancement of the qualities associated with its location. Should a square surround a break in a line, for example, it implies that whatever problem is signified by the break will be overcome without detriment to the further functioning of that line.

A cross may be considered as favourable or unfavourable depending on its location. It may be regarded as an interference mark similar in effect to that of a bar or grille should it appear on a line or mount.

However, a clearly defined and completely independent cross formation seen in the space between head and heart lines – the mystic cross – signifies an inclination towards spiritual, philosophical or metaphysical matters. The owner of this mark may simply be interested in such subjects or may develop and utilise the talents associated with them.

A similar, independently formed cross, in this case between the fate and life lines, three or four centimetres above the wrist, is known as the life-saving cross and marks a great concern for others' welfare. It is sometimes found in the hands of someone whose occupation provides opportunities to help other people physically or psychologically.

Other small incidental marks that may be found in the hands include the circle, star and triangle. Their possible locations and interpretations are too numerous to list here (besides which, opinions seem to vary widely), so I can only suggest further reading for those who are especially interested in the subject.

Perfect circles are, in fact, rarely seen and may be confused with islands if on a line. In very general terms, circles may be regarded as favourable except on the Luna mount; stars are considered beneficial except at the end of a line and triangles tend to enhance the qualities of the mounts on which they are usually found.

Another mark worth mentioning occurs on the top phalange of the fingers where a series of small horizontal lines may be seen. These are known as white lines because they show up as such on hand-prints and signify a depletion of natural energy, probably due to overwork, stress, lack of sufficient rest or poor diet.

This marking will soon fade once a sensible regime is resumed but, should the subject fail to change his/her life style, the health may suffer. Whatever happens to be the weakest point in the constitution will deteriorate under the strain, so a change of attitude is advisable.

The Quadrangle and Great Triangle

The area of palm between head and heart lines is known as the quadrangle and, ideally, this should be free from any influence lines other than the fate and Sun lines which may cross it.

If the head and heart lines run parallel, the space between will be of uniform appearance, denoting a well-balanced personality; the wider the gap, the more extrovert the nature; the narrower the gap, the more reticent the individual is likely to be. When an irregularly shaped quadrangle is formed due to the heart line dipping down to a normally positioned head line, it points to a predominantly emotional character whereas a high-set head line indicates a more impersonal outlook.

Another palmar area which should be clearly defined and relatively free of influence lines is the great triangle. This lies below the quadrangle and is normally bounded by the head, life and Mercury lines. Again, a narrow formation implies a cautious nature whereas a wide angle between head and life lines suggests the reverse.

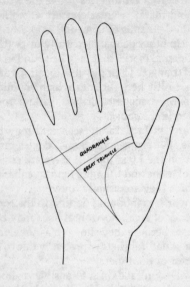

5   Dating Events

The whole concept of dating events on the lines of the hand poses problems, not the least of which is what to do if, for instance, there isn't a fate line on the subject's hand or the life line stops short after a few centimetres. Another hoary chestnut concerns the heart line and on which side of the hand it begins and ends.

One major problem is that the traditional methods of timing events on the hands are all based on the assumption that people live only for the biblical three score years and ten. This may indeed have been the case during the period when such methods were devised, but it certainly isn't so now with the advent of modern medical care, better nutrition and a generally higher standard of living.

So, for those who want them, the traditional divisions of time on the major lines of the hand are illustrated here. However, they should not go unremarked. *(See page 96)*.

Importantly, in view of the longer life expectancy nowadays, I would suggest that the divisions marked should be regarded as representing twelve years instead of ten. This would extend the 'allotted span' to a more realistic 84, so would seem an acceptable adjustment to make. To that end, the suggested alternatives are shown in brackets alongside the original figures.

The other important point to make is that no matter what method is used, it should be regarded as a guide and not as an absolute. Always compare the actual hand under study to the timing chart being used to verify whether or not the dates seem to coincide fairly well.

For instance, if the person concerned had a major heart operation at the age of 40 and this is obvious from the marks on the hands, note the position of these on the actual hand and then identify the corresponding points on your guide sheet to gauge how far out it is. In this way it should be possible to get a fairly accurate idea of how timing can be estimated on that particular hand.

It won't, however, necessarily coincide with the next hand you study, so each hand should be treated separately and individually, using major

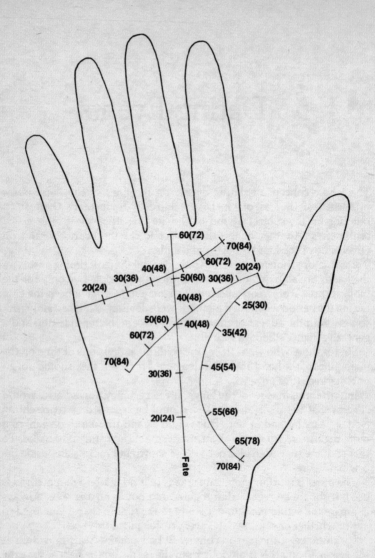

events in the subject's life as pegs on which to base your estimates.

Incidentally, in purely practical terms, it is much easier to use hand-prints and a pair of dividers when comparing distances as this is much more accurate than relying on observation alone.

6   Hand-Prints

Although it is obviously possible to study a person's hands without taking prints, it is not easy to distinguish the finer details, especially of the lines, without doing so even if using a magnifying-glass. It is therefore important to take prints if the intention is to give a full analysis because any assessment can only be as accurate as the information on which it is based.

Also, the lines on the hands alter to reflect changes in the individual's attitudes, style of life, health fluctuations and so on; only the skin-ridge patterns remain constant throughout life. Taking hand-prints at regular intervals will enable such changes to be recorded as they occur, thus making it easier to predict future trends. Hand-prints will also provide invaluable data for anyone who wishes to build up his/her knowledge of palmistry.

Equipment

Many people are put off taking prints because they believe that complicated equipment or expensive materials are needed, yet this is not the case. If the 'ideal' equipment is not readily to hand, it is very easy to improvise. So, what is needed?

First, of course, paper of some sort on which to make the prints. It doesn't matter what sort of paper you use as long as the sheets are large enough to accommodate a spread-out hand comfortably. A4 sheets are ideal and smooth paper is preferable to a rough-textured one which may be too absorbent.

Something to take the prints with is the next requirement and almost anything that isn't too messy yet will not dry too quickly can be used.

Ideally, black water-based lino ink will make good clear prints and is easy to wash off the hands. Finger-print ink, printer's ink, poster paints, etc. can all be used, even lipstick in an emergency, but these will not be so easy to remove afterwards.

A small roller about 4 in. wide is needed for spreading the ink on the hand. The hard rubber ones used by photographers and artists are ideal or it is usually possible to find suitable alternatives in hardware stores or decorating shops.

Finally, a smooth, washable surface on which to spread the ink. This may be a small sheet of heavy glass, about 12 in. square, a large glazed tile, formica work surface or perhaps one of those plastic coated saucepan stands that most people seem to have in their kitchens.

Method

There are several methods of taking prints, but the initial preparations are the same:

1 Squeeze an inch or two of the water-based ink out of its tube on to the glass sheet.
2 Using the roller, work it backwards and forwards until the ink has an even consistency.
3 Ink the hand, working the roller in one direction only, starting about an inch or so below the wrist right up to the finger-tips. Make sure you ink the sides of the fingers and edges of the palm or you won't get a print of the whole hand.

The hand is now ready for taking a print and this is the point where the alternative methods begin:

Method A – Seat the subject comfortably at a table or desk covered with a cloth or towel (to prevent the paper sliding about when the prints are being taken) and place a large sheet of paper almost up to the edge of the table in front of him/her.

Ask him to place his hand down firmly on the paper in one movement while you hold the edges to keep it in position. Apply firm pressure to the back of his hand, fingers, thumb and wrist areas. Transfer your grip to the top and bottom of the paper and hold if firmly while the subject raises his hand straight up vertically in one movement.

You should have a good, clean print and it only remains to shift the paper right up to the edge of the table and ask the subject to press his thumb down on it with your fingers pressing on top to prevent slipping.

Method B – Ink the hand and place the paper in position as before. Then position the subject's hand about 12 in. above the paper. Hold the paper very firmly by its edges and ask him to slap his hand down on the paper swiftly and firmly: straight down and up again immediately. Again, complete the print by adding the thumb print by the normal method.

Method C – This method requires an additional piece of equipment, a rolling pin. Yes, that's right, an ordinary kitchen rolling-pin, preferably one with handles. This method produces by far the best results but it does require practice as you are the one who has to be in control and the person whose hand is being printed inevitably tries to 'help' – with unsuccessful results. So do get the subject to practice the movements needed before inking his hands, he'll soon get the idea.

Ink the hand as before. Place the rolling-pin at arm's length from the subject in front of him on the table. Place a sheet of paper on the rolling-pin and hold both in position with one hand while grasping the subject's wrist with the other. Position his wrist on top of the rolling-pin, near the bottom edge of the paper.

Now get him to roll his hand back slowly towards him while you hold the paper on the rolling-pin. There is no need to apply a great deal of pressure but just before the pin rolls out from beneath the paper, get him to stop briefly and gently press the ends of his fingers and thumb down to ensure these print out properly. He should then lift his hand swiftly from the paper while you hold everything else in position. Again, add the thumb print in the usual way.

Method D – This is a method that is quite useful if the subject is infirm or disabled. Ink the hand as before and place it palm up on the mat or towel. Lay a sheet of paper on the inked hand and roll a clean roller across the surface of the paper so that the print forms on the underside of the sheet. Finally, remove the paper carefully from the hand by peeling it back smoothly so as not to smudge the print. Take the thumb print separately.

It does take practice to get good results and it is more difficult to print some hands than others due to individual physical characteristics. So always take several prints of both hands on each occasion so that you can select the best of the batch and always remember to date and identify the prints in the corner of the sheet or on the back for future reference and possible comparison.

To judge whether a print is of an acceptable standard or not, look at the lines on the palm and fingertips. These should be clearly visible under a good magnifying-glass and will be invaluable for detailed analysis.

Whichever method is used, it is important to realise that the prints obtained are 'negatives' of the hand. The white lines on the print are the lines on the hand; a print showing the thumb to the left of the palm is really a print of the right hand and vice versa.

7   Assessing the Data

Before studying the hand prints it is useful to note certain physical characteristics of the hands themselves if at all possible. First, look at the back of the hands, compare their size and shape; take note of any outstanding features such as extreme hairiness; skin-texture and colour; the position and length of the fingers and thumbs; the shape and condition of the nails; and the presence or absence of moons.

Feel the hands: are they stiff and unyielding; does the flesh spring back under pressure; are they hard and horny or soft and flabby? All such apparently minor details will help build up a 'profile' of the person whose hands are under study.

Once you have gleaned all the information possible from the backs and general structure of the hands, look at the palms. Note the development or otherwise of the mounts, feeling them between your fingers and thumb if necessary, and especially if the palms are bony.

Note, too, the general appearance of the lines: are they firmly and deeply etched or faintly scratched on the surface; do they look too faint and shallow for the hand they are on or are they ridiculously broad and deep? Are the hands relatively free of small influence lines and stress marks or are they covered with a fine tracery of lines? And what about the thumbs, do they 'belong' to the hands or do they look out of place; are they low or high set?

Ask the subject to hold his/her hands up in the air with palms towards you, as if someone were pointing a gun at him: note the finger setting and the angle the thumb makes to the hand. Are the fingers held tightly together or are they splayed out; do the thumbs bend right back towards the wrists or are they stiff and straight?

Don't be afraid to feel the hands, sometimes the only way of gauging mount development is by touch and flexibility must, of course, be tested manually. Very flexible fingers will bend back at the top joints very easily with just a little manipulation and very pliable hands will yield easily to pressure at the knuckle joints.

Don't forget, either, to compare left and right hands as this is of prime importance in determining where the subject's best efforts are concentrated and where potentialities remain untapped. The dominant, active or objective hand – the one normally used for writing, wielding tools etc. – should be better developed physically than the passive hand and, very often, its lines will be more clearly defined and deeply etched.

If this is not the case and the left hand of a naturally right-handed person, for instance, is the more capable and stronger looking of the two, it implies that he has not realised his resources fully. Perhaps the subject has not yet explored or exploited his underlying talents due to lack of initiative or maybe his confidence needs a bit of a boost.

Whatever the reason, pointing out the potential shown in someone's hands may provide the incentive for him to make the extra effort required to put his inherent talents to better use. So, a comparison of left and right hands will help both you and the subject to understand to what extent individuality has overcome the restrictions of childhood and the limitations imposed by his current environment and life style.

With practice, you will quickly learn to note all such details as have been mentioned automatically and will probably develop a form of shorthand for jotting down aide-memoires on the back of the prints. At first though, and certainly if you think you are likely to take up palmistry seriously, it may be quite a good idea to devise a fact sheet on which all these finer points can be recorded and keep this with the hand prints. It will then be a simple matter to refer to the fact sheet and refresh your memory should you wish to reconsider the original prints or compare them to later ones to see just how the subject's life style has altered as his personality develops. Simply as a guide, I would suggest something on the lines of the example on *page 100* but you are, naturally, at liberty to adapt it to suit your particular needs or preferences.

It is quite fascinating to observe the changes that take place in the hands, so a collection of hand prints taken six months apart in the case of a child or perhaps at yearly intervals for an older person, can be very revealing. It is also of course much easier to offer guidance or advice if one has previous material on which to base one's estimate of the direction that an individual's life is following at any given time.

If, though, you notice any serious health indications, do remember that you are not a medical practitioner and refer the subject to his doctor for professional advice. Minor problems – such as poor sleeping habits – may, quite simply, be caused by stress and, if so, this will show plainly in the hands. In such cases, of course, it would be only sensible to advise the subject to slow down and take more care of diet and amount of sleep.

Even if you don't intend to become a practising palmist, a study of the hands can prove an absorbing and rewarding hobby.

Sample Fact Sheet

	LEFT HAND	RIGHT HAND
NAME: AGE: DATE PRINTS TAKEN: DOMINANT HAND:		
BASIC SHAPE		
BACK OF HAND		
Consistency: Texture/Colour: Knuckles: Nails: Outstanding Features		
FINGERS		
Classification: Tips: Flexibility: Setting/Spacing: Other Features:		
THUMBS		
Classification: Phalange Dominance: Flexibility: Setting/Angle: Other Features:		
MOUNTS		
Jupiter: Saturn: Apollo: Mercury: Venus: Luna: Neptune: Mars Upper: Mars Lower: Plain of Mars:		
ADDITIONAL COMMENTS		

Index